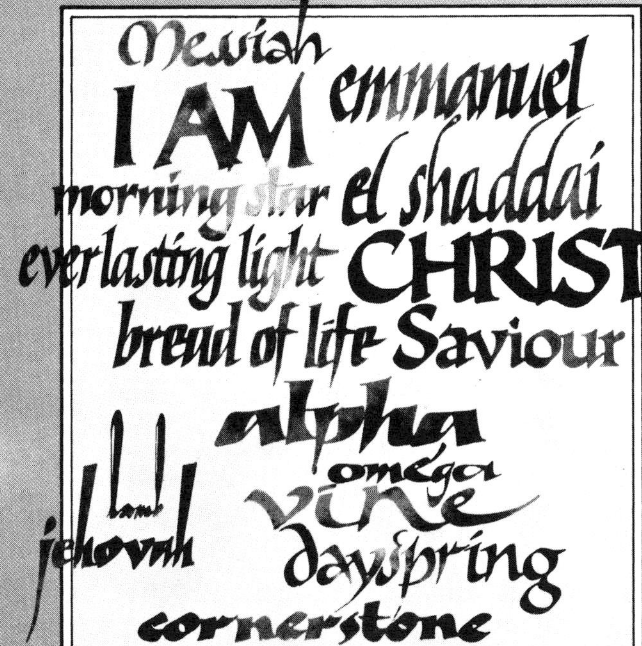

Group Study Guide

FOR

SUNDAY SCHOOL AND SMALL GROUPS

ACCENT PUBLICATIONS
Colorado Springs, Colorado

Accent Publications
4050 Lee Vance View
P.O. Box 36640
Colorado Springs, Colorado 80936

Printed in the United States of America

Library of Congress Catalog Card Number 92-73211

ISBN 0-89636-289-2

Third Printing

Contents

It's okay to copy pages of this book if:

- ☛ you photocopy only the pages designated by the statement, "Permission granted to reproduce."
- ☛ you or someone else in your church or organization are the original purchaser.
- ☛ you are using the copies you make for a non-commercial purpose such as teaching or promoting another ministry within your church or ministry organization.
- ☛ the material copied is not combined with any other author's work in any other written or printed form, published or non-published.

However, it is illegal to make copies if:

- ☛ the material copied is used to promote, advertise, or sell another product or service.
- ☛ the material copied is used in or on another product which will be sold.
- ☛ you or your organization are not the original purchaser of this book.
- ☛ the material is not used in your church or ministry organization for the purpose intended.

This Group Study Guide is a valuable resource for the Leader of church Bible study groups, Sunday School classes, home Bible studies—any place a group of "students" meet to zero in on a specific Bible study topic.

The Bible commentary on this study is found in the Accent book, *The Names of Jesus* by Dr. Elmer L. Towns. It is imperative that each Leader secures a copy of the Accent book in order to teach the course. It is also important for each group member to have a personal copy of *The Names of Jesus* so that he or she will receive the personal, practical benefits of the study.

I. HOW TO USE THE STUDY GUIDE

The first part of each session's material is tailor-made to that specific study. First you will find applicable *Bible Verses*, followed by *Study Goals*, *Materials Needed*, and suggestions for *Advance Preparation.*

Following these helpful suggestions is an *A B C Plan for the Study*, giving the Leader an easy format to use to each:

A – Approach

B – Bible Exploration

C – Conclusion

Each section is designed to help produce maximum learning and practical application in the lives of the Study Group participants.

II. STUDY OUTLINES FOR GROUP PARTICIPANTS

There is a Study Outline for each of the 12 sessions which can be given as handouts to the group participants. They will enable each group member to take notes as the lesson is presented.

III. DISCUSSION SHEETS FOR GROUP PARTICIPANTS

These handouts give tangible assignments to group members to enhance their study. The Discussion Sheets also include a list of the chapters from the Gospels as suggested reading for the week. By following these suggestions, everyone will have read through the four Gospels at the end of the 12-session study.

IV. JOURNALING

An additional tool included for those involved in the study is "How to Keep a Daily Journal of Your Christian Life." This is a one-time handout to the group members. Throughout the study, the Leader should encourage group members to be consistent in journaling as an avenue of spiritual growth.

With the resources and practical applications tailored to each session, you, as Leader of the study group, will pave the way for each participant to come to know Jesus as Lord, Friend, Provider, Intercessor, Coming King—and much more!

NOTES:

Study 1

The Name of Jesus

A B C Plan for the Study

Study Verse:

"And she shall bring forth a son, and thou shalt call his name JESUS: for he shall save his people from their sins" (Matthew 1:21).

Study Goals:

1. To help group members gain a better understanding of the meaning of the name "Jesus."
2. To help group members experience ongoing growth in their relationship with their Saviour.

Materials Needed:

1. Copies of the Accent book, *The Names of Jesus*, by Elmer L. Towns for group members to purchase.
2. One copy of the Study 1 Lesson Outline for each group member.
3. One copy of the Lesson 1 Discussion Sheet to be distributed to each participant at the beginning of the session. (You may wish to hand out Discussion Sheets the week prior to each study so group members have time to work on them before the study).
4. One copy of *How to Keep a Daily Journal of Your Christian Life.* This is a one-time handout for each group member. It should be passed out at the beginning of the study series.

Advance Preparation:

1. As you prepare to lead/teach this series, take time to review this Leader's Guide to gain a clear perspective on your objectives in this study series.
2. If possible, distribute the Accent book, *The Names of Jesus,* to group members before your first session together and encourage them to read chapter one.
3. Photocopy one copy of the article *How to Keep a Daily Journal of Your Christian Life* for each member of your group.
4. Write various names of Jesus on construction paper and display them appropriately at the front of your room. Leave these names up throughout the series or replace them from time to

time with new names. Refer to the appendix in the Accent book for names you may wish to consider.

Approach

1. Begin the study series in an informal way by making the group members conscious of "names." Have each group member introduce himself/herself to the group and share one "nickname" they picked up as a child or in their workplace environment. He or she may wish to explain briefly how that name was acquired and suggest whether it is, at least in part, an accurate description.
2. Introduce this session by reminding group members that names often describe something specific about the person to whom they are applied. As we study the names of Jesus in this series, our goal will be to get to know the Lord we love more intimately.

Bible Exploration

Step 1: *Lecture*

1. Distribute a copy of the Study 1 Lesson Outline to each group member. This outline is designed to encourage note taking during this session together. Mention that outlines will be available for each succeeding study.
2. Explain how both Paul and Moses expressed the desire of many Christians today to know God better (Philippians 3:10; Exodus 33:13). We grow in our knowledge of God as we grow in our understanding of His names (Exodus 34:5).
3. Dr. Towns writes, "*A devout Moslem exhausts his knowledge of his god when he knows the ninety-nine names and attributes of Allah in the Koran. But the Bible identifies more than 700 descriptive names and titles of Jesus Christ.*"
4. Share with group members the special status before God which belongs to "them that feared the Lord, and that thought upon his name" (Malachi 3:16).
5. Conclude by suggesting the Pauline description "Our Lord Jesus Christ" summarizes who Jesus is with reference to His title, name and office. Explain that this session will focus on His name, Jesus.
6. Present a review of the first chapter using the following outline:

   A. The Meaning of His Identification
      1. The name Jesus/Joshua means "Jehovah the Saviour."
      2. When applied to Joshua in the Old Testament, it was an expression of faith in Jehovah's purpose to save His people.

Notes:

NOTES:

3. When applied to Jesus in the New Testament, it was an expression of the nature of Jesus. He was "Jehovah the Saviour."

B. The Mystery of His Incarnation

1. Jesus was so named because He was "God in the flesh."
2. The means by which God became a man involved the miracle of the virgin birth.

C. The Marvels of His Occupation

1. As "Jehovah the Saviour," Jesus' primary work was the saving of His people from their sins.
2. The extent of His saving work was first recognized by the Samaritans who identified Him as "the Saviour of the World."

D. The Majesty of His Reputation

1 God has given Jesus "a name which is above every name."
2. As Christians, we have a moral responsibility to "live up to the name of Jesus."
3. In prayer, Christians should pray "in Jesus' name" which means to pray on the basis of Jesus' merit rather than their own.
4. There is a unique spiritual power in the name of Jesus.
5. The name of Jesus is a worthy object of our worship and meditation.

STEP 2: *Discussion*

Use the following questions as a basis for your discussion of chapter one. (The questions for discussion are also included on the last page of each chapter of *The Names of Jesus*.

1. What does the name Jesus mean? Why was it popular when Joseph and Mary gave it to their Son?
2. Why did parents discontinue naming their sons Jesus? What does this teach us about our attitude toward the name of Jesus?
3. What does it mean to "live up to the name of Jesus"?
4. Should we end our prayers by saying "in Jesus' name"? Why or why not?
5. Name your favorite hymn about Jesus. Why is it your favorite hymn?

STEP 3: *Journaling*

1. Throughout the history of the Christian church, many have used the discipline of journaling as a means of recording growth in their Christian life. Distribute copies of the article, "How to Keep a Daily Journal of Your Christian Life," and briefly review

its contents. Encourage group members to use this study series to begin developing this discipline in their own lives.

2. Explain that if group members read a chapter a day from the Gospels as suggested on each week's Discussion Sheet, they will read all four Gospels during the 12 weeks of this study series. Encourage group members to begin reading Matthew this week. As they read, they should look for the names ascribed to Jesus in each chapter. Then choose one name as the basis of that day's journal entry.
3. Inform group members that during the last session in this study series, they will be encouraged to share their thoughts on a particular name out of their journal with the rest of the group.

NOTES:

III Conclusion

1. The name of Jesus is the theme of many hymns and choruses which may be familiar to members of your group. Choose one to sing together as you bring this session to a close.
2. Encourage group members to be consistent in their reading of the suggested Bible chapters each week (reading one chapter per day), looking for and recording the various names and titles of Jesus used in that Gospel.

Assignments:

1. Members prepare for the next study by reading chapter two in *The Names of Jesus*.
2. Encourage group members to begin reading through Matthew at a rate of one chapter per day looking for the various names and titles of Jesus used in that Gospel. This daily reading should serve as the basis of their journaling.

NOTES:

The Title "Lord"

A B C Plan for the Study

Study Verses:

"For unto you is born this day in the city of David a Saviour, which is Christ the Lord" (Luke 2:11).

"Therefore let all the house of Israel know assuredly, that God hath made that same Jesus, whom ye crucified, both Lord and Christ" (Acts 2:36).

"That if thou shalt confess with thy mouth the Lord Jesus, and shalt believe in thine heart that God hath raised him from the dead, thou shalt be saved" (Romans 10:9).

Study Goals:

1. To help group members better understand the implications of the title "Lord" as applied to Jesus.
2. To help group members yield more fully to the lordship of Christ in their individual life.

Materials Needed:

1. Copies of *The Names of Jesus* by Elmer L. Towns.
2. One copy of the Study 2 Lesson Outline and Discussion Sheet for each group member.
3. Assorted books about Jesus from your church library or on consignment from your local Christian bookstore. These books should be related to the themes of chapters four through 12 in the book, *The Names of Jesus*.

Advance Preparation:

1. Set up a table of books dealing with the themes of chapters four through 12 in *The Names of Jesus*. This table should be set up prior to group members arrival so they will have time to browse before and after this study session.
2. Have copies of the student handout, *"How to Keep a Daily Journal of Your Christian Life,"* available for group members who missed the last session.

Approach

NOTES:

1. Begin by asking group members to think of a one word description of someone in an authority role in their life (i.e. a parent, employer, etc.). These words should accurately describe the relationship they have with that person.
2. Explain that this session examines the meaning of the title "Lord," one of the most common titles of Jesus used in Scripture to describe Him and our relationship to Him.
3. Encourage the group members to begin reading through the Gospels and write a daily entry in their journal based on a name of Jesus in that day's chapter.

Bible Exploration

Step 1: *Personal Testimony*

1. The author begins this chapter with an account of how his title has changed throughout his teaching career. Share how people have addressed you differently (by different names or titles) throughout your personal career. If this does not apply to you, have another group member share or review the author's illustration.

Step 2: *Lecture*

1. Distribute a copy of the Study 2 Lesson Outline and Discussion Sheet to each group member.
2. The expression "Lord Jesus" occurs 115 times in the New Testament. Many of these verses describe how Jesus relates to us as Lord in different areas of our lives. Prepare a brief lecture based on chapter two of *The Names of Jesus* or your own study of the biblical use of the expression "Lord Jesus." The focus of this lecture should show how Jesus relates to us as Lord in different aspects of our experience.
3. Present a review of the second chapter using the following outline:

   A. The Meaning of This Name

      1. The Greek word *kurios* translated "Lord" is used in the New Testament to describe an owner (Luke 19:33), one who has disposal of anything (Matthew 12:8), a master to whom service is due (Matthew 6:24), an emperor or king (Acts 25:26; Revelation 17:14), a father (Matthew 21:30), husband (I Peter 3:6), master (Matthew 13:27), ruler (Matthew 27:63), angel (Acts 10:4), a stranger (Acts 16:30), a pagan idol or deity (I Corinthians 8:5), and the Old Testament name of God (*Jehovah* - Matthew 4:7; *Adonai* - Matthew 1:22; *Elohim* - I Peter 1:25).

NOTES:

2. When this title is ascribed to Jesus, it recognizes His (a) right to respect, (b) right to be served, (c) right of disposal, and (d) right to rule and hold authority over others.
3. This title implies Jesus' absolute control in the lives of His disciples. Compare the contrast between the use of "Master" and "Lord" by Peter (Luke 5:5-8) and the disciples (Matthew 26:22-25).
4. Thomas used the expression "my Lord and my God" (John 20:28) to affirm His faith in Jesus. This was also the constant theme of apostolic preaching (II Corinthians 4:5).

B. The Message of This Name

1. The title "Lord" is closely related to what it means to be a Christian (Romans 10:9).
2. Recognizing the Lordship of Christ is a work of the Holy Spirit in our life (I Corinthians 12:3) which we need to recognize and apply personally (I Peter 3:15; Romans 12:1).
3. The essence of Christian stewardship is recognizing the Lordship of Christ over everything (Psalms 24:1).
4. Lordship means "absolute surrender" to the will of God.
5. Lordship is applied practically in our life in four steps.
    a. Knowing the doctrinal basis of our victory in the Christian life, i.e. our union with Christ (Romans 6:3, 6, 9).
    b. Reckoning or relying on that fact to be true in our experience (Romans 6:11).
    c. Yielding to His Lordship "once and for all" (Romans 6:13, 16, 19).
    d. Obeying Christ as an expression of our yieldedness to His will (Romans 6:16, 17).

STEP 3: *Discussion*

Use the following questions as a basis for your discussion of chapter two.

1. What did the word "Lord" mean in the culture of our Saviour's day?
2. Explain the term "Lordship of Christ."
3. Can you recall a time when you surrendered your life to the Lord? (Have two or three group members share briefly.)
4. Explain the statement: "Jesus is the Lord of your life whether you let Him operate in your life or not."
5. Where will you be when "everyone" recognizes the Lordship of Christ? (You may wish to ask this as a rhetorical question.)

III Conclusion

NOTES:

1. Dr. Towns writes, *"Paul uses four key verbs in Romans 6 which describe various aspects of what it means to call Jesus 'Lord'. The words are* know, reckon, yield, *and* obey. *These are keys to the victorious Christian life."* (See page 28 of *The Names of Jesus.*)
2. Lead group members through a brief study of Romans 6, highlighting these four key verbs. Have group members complete the Discussion Sheet chart, *Yielding to the Lord,* as you guide this part of the study.
3. Ask each group member to think of one area of his or her life which needs to be yielded to the Lord. Then review the chart, helping them learn how to yield that aspect of their life to the Lord.
4. Conclude the session with a time of silent prayer. Invite group members to take a first step by telling God they want Jesus to be Lord of every area of their lives. End this part of the lesson by praying that God would help each one present experience the Lordship of Jesus in a fresh way this week.
5. Remind group members of the books on the browsing table. Explain that you would like several group members to share a brief review of a book to introduce a future session.

Assignments:

1. Members prepare for the next study by reading chapter three in *The Names of Jesus.*
2. Enlist nine group members to prepare a brief book review for future sessions. The book reviewed each week will be related to the theme of that session (sessions four through 12). If you have a smaller group, enlist five group members to prepare book reviews for sessions four, six, eight, ten and 12.
3. Encourage group members to continue reading through Matthew and making journal entries.

NOTES:

The Office of Christ

A B C Plan for the Study

Study Verse:

"Come, see a man, which told me all things that ever I did: is not this the Christ?" (John 4:29).

Study Goals:

1. To help group members grasp the full meaning implied in the office of *Christ*.
2. To help group members experience a richer communion with Christ based on a deeper understanding of their union with God "in Christ."

Materials Needed:

1. Copies of the book, *The Names of Jesus*, by Elmer L. Towns.
2. One copy of the Study 3 Lesson Outline and Discussion Sheet for each group member.

Advance Preparation:

1. At the conclusion of this lesson, assign special research reports to various members of your study group. Take time this week to think about which group member to ask to prepare a report for each chapter left in the book.
2. Write out several of the 76 New Testament verses which include the expression "in Christ" on pieces of construction paper shaped like a ram's horn. You may wish to enlist the assistance of other group members who are willing to be more involved but do not want to give a report.

Approach

1. Hang the ram's horn "in Christ" mobiles from the ceiling in the room where your study group meets. They should be low enough so group members can read the verses. Encourage each group member to take time to examine the mobiles as they arrive.

2. Distribute a copy of Study 3 Lesson Outline and Discussion Sheet to each group member as they arrive.
3. Begin this session by briefly summarizing the relationship between the words "Messiah" and "Christ" and their common root meaning (the anointed one).

NOTES:

III Bible Exploration

STEP 1: *Bible Search*

1. Ask group members to look up the following verses to identify the offices into which the subject was being anointed: Exodus 29:7; I Samuel 16:13; I Kings 19:16.

STEP 2: *Discussion*

Use the following questions as a basis for your discussion of chapter three.

1. What is the literal meaning of the name Christ? Why do you think it was Paul's favorite name for the Saviour?
2. How did Christ fulfill His office as prophet?
3. As an anointed priest, how does Christ minister to us today?
4. Describe the kingdom and rule of Jesus Christ, the King.
5. God's Word teaches that believers are "in Christ" and Christ abides in believers. What effect does this have on your everyday life?

STEP 3: *Promises for Living*

1. Ask group members to pull down an anointing horn mobile with an "in Christ" reference which is especially meaningful to them.
2. Have each group member share what their verse teaches we all have "in Christ."
3. You may wish to take time to encourage group members to share other things we all have "in Christ."
4. Present a review of the third chapter using the following outline:
   A. The Messiah in the Old Testament
      1. Like Moses, the Messiah was viewed as an anointed Prophet (Deuteronomy 18:15-19). What makes a prophet a prophet? Prophets were called:
         a. "The Man of God" emphasizing his relationship to God, his message from God, and his godly character.
         b. "The Servant of God" expressing their willingness to obey God and involvement in the ministry of prayer.

NOTES:

c. "The Prophet (*Nabi')*" which is derived from the verb "to call." The prophet was one who was called of God.

d. "The Seer (*Ro'eh/Hozeh*)" which stresses their vision.

e. The Greek verb *prophaino* means "to reveal" and includes both predicting the future and revealing God's message.

f. The Greek verb *prothemi* means "to tell forth" as one who declares God's message.

g. The prophet was a "For-teller" (Spokesman for God), "Foreteller" (Predictor of future events), and "Forth-teller" (Preacher to people).

2. Like Melchizedek, the Messiah was viewed as an anointed Priest (Psalm 110:4). What made a priest a priest?
   a. He was called of God to this ministry.
   b. He represented others before God.
   c. He offered the sacrifice for sin.
   d. He prayed on behalf of others (intercession).
3. Like David, the Messiah was viewed as an anointed King (II Samuel 16:13). How do we recognize the kingship of Jesus?
   a. His kingship is derived from His deity (I Timothy 1:17).
   b. As King, He has a kingdom (John 18:36).
   c. If Jesus is our King, we are His subjects (Luke 17:10).

B. The Christ in the New Testament
1. Although Jesus never used this title of Himself, He commended those who did (Matthew 16:16, 17). It is most probable that those who used this expression in the Gospels and early chapters of Acts did so with the Old Testament anointed offices in mind.
2. One of the major themes in the writings of Paul is that of the union of Christ and the believer. He uses the expression "in Christ" 172 times to express this thought.
3. Our union with Christ refers to our non-experiential state or position in heaven as believers.
4. Our communion with Christ refers to our experiential realization of the intimate relationship we already have with Christ.
5. Distribute several "ram's horns" and have group members share the promise to those who are "in Christ."

III Conclusion

1. Take time at the conclusion of this lesson so each group member can share in a time of prayer thanking God for what they have "in Christ." If you are leading a large group, you may want to

break up into smaller groups to ensure greater involvement in this part of the session.

2. Explain that the remaining sessions in this study series will focus on name groupings rather than on an individual name of Jesus. Enroll individuals to prepare special reports on the significance of each name group which will be presented each week. If you have a smaller group, enlist four group members to prepare reports for sessions five, seven, nine and eleven.

Assignments:

1. Members prepare for the next study by reading chapter four in *The Names of Jesus*.
2. Contact the group member(s) presenting the book report and/or special report during the next week to remind them of their involvement in the lesson.
3. Encourage group members to be consistent in their journal entries as they finish reading the Gospel of Matthew this week.

NOTES:

NOTES:

The Old Testament Prophetic Names of Jesus

A B C Plan for the Study

Study Verses:

"Philip findeth Nathanael, and saith unto him, We have found him of whom Moses in the law, and the prophets, did write, Jesus of Nazareth, the son of Joseph" (John 1:45).

"And beginning at Moses and all the prophets, he expounded unto them, in all the scriptures the things concerning himself" (Luke 24:27).

Study Goals:

1. To help group members learn some of the principal Old Testament prophetic names of Jesus.
2. To help group members appreciate in Jesus what the prophets could only anticipate.

Materials Needed:

1. Copies of *The Names of Jesus* by Elmer L. Towns.
2. One copy of the Study 4 Lesson Outline and Discussion Sheet for each group member.

Advance Preparation:

1. Contact the group member(s) presenting the book review and/ or special report to remind them of their involvement in this week's session.
2. Replace some of the names of Jesus in your room with new names which tie in more closely with this week's theme: the Old Testament prophetic names of Jesus.
3. Arrange to have the tape, record, or compact disk player set up and ready to go before class members arrive.

Approach

1. Have music playing as group members arrive to help set a mood for studying the Old Testament names of God. You may wish to

play songs that feature these names, have a distinctive Jewish flavor in their melody or selections from something like Handel's *Messiah*.

2. Distribute a copy of the Study 4 Lesson Outline and Discussion Sheet to group members as they arrive.
3. Begin this session with the statement, *"The Old Testament is Christ concealed. The New Testament is Christ revealed."*
4. Explain that the purpose of this session is to look at some of the Old Testament prophetic names of Jesus.

III Bible Exploration

Step 1: *Book Review*

1. In session two, you assigned a group member to prepare a brief book review. Have him or her introduce the book chosen and share briefly about the book. Use the suggested book review outline form given in Discussion Sheet 2 as a guide for presenting the book.
2. If there is significant interest in the book on the part of other group members, let the reviewer field two or three questions from group members before moving on.

Step 2: *Special Report*

1. In session three, you assigned a group member to prepare a special report on the theme of this chapter. Have this group member share briefly his or her findings with the rest of the group. The reporter should include his or her favorite Old Testament name of Jesus and explain briefly the reasons for that choice.

Step 3: *Discussion*

Use the following questions as a basis for your discussion of chapter four.

1. What is probably the earliest name of Christ in the Old Testament? What do we know about our Saviour from this title?
2. One of the favorite titles for Christ used by the prophets was Branch. How is Christ our Branch?
3. Haggai called Christ "the desire of all nations." How does Christ fulfill this title?
4. Isaiah called Christ "the ensign of the people." What should be our reaction to this name?
5. Share an experience when you realized that Christ is your *El Shaddai*.

Notes:

NOTES:

STEP 4: *Review*

1. Present a review of this chapter using the following outline:

   A. Shiloh means "peace maker" and refers to Jesus as the one who makes peace between God and humanity (Genesis 49:10; Isaiah 9:6).

   B. Prophet - Review "What makes a prophet a prophet?" from last week's session.

   C. Branch (*Netzer*)

      1. This title may refer to the negative reputation Jesus bore based on His childhood home (Matthew 2:23; Isaiah 14:19).

      2. The four Gospels emphasize four aspects of the Branch-character of Jesus (Matthew - David a righteous Branch [Jeremiah 23:5]; Mark - My servant the Branch [Zechariah 3:8]; Luke - the man whose name is the Branch [Zechariah 6:12]; John - the Branch of the Lord [Isaiah 4:2]).

   D. Desire of All Nations

      1. According to Jewish commentators, the second temple lacked five things: (a) the ark of the covenant with its mercy seat, (b) the tables of the law, (c) the holy fire, (d) the urim and thummim, and (e) the Shekinah glory of God.

      2. As the Desire of All Nations, Jesus visited that temple. He was Himself (a) the propitiation for our sins (I John 2:2), (b) the Lawgiver (James 4:12), (c) the Wall of Fire (Zechariah 2:5), (d) the Urim and Thummim (Exodus 28:30), and (e) the Glory of the Father (John 1:14).

   E. Ensign of the Peoples is the flag which brings all believers from all places together.

   F. *El Shaddai* - The Almighty

      1. *El Shaddai* describes "the mother-love of God."

      2. *El Shaddai* has been translated "The God who is Enough."

      3. *El Shaddai* was Job's favorite name for God implying God supplied what was needed to comfort Job's pain.

2. Sometimes people argue that the God of the Old Testament is different from the God of the New Testament. Take one of these Old Testament names and share how you have found it relevant in your Christian life during the past six months.

3. Remind group members that the Old Testament names of Jesus have New Testament meanings in the Christian life.

III Conclusion

1. Sometimes it is argued that the God of the Old Testament is different from the God of the New Testament. Ask group members to share how a particular Old Testament prophetic name of Jesus has a New Testament meaning for the Christian life today.
2. Have several group members share a favorite Old Testament name of Jesus and the reason for that choice.
3. As you end this session in prayer, lead your group in appreciation for the contribution of the Old Testament to our fuller understanding of who Jesus is.

Assignments:

1. Members prepare for the next study by reading chapter five in *The Names of Jesus.*
2. Contact the group member(s) presenting the book report and/ or special report next week to remind them of their involvement in the lesson.
3. Encourage group members to continue their journaling. This week would be a good time for those who didn't make it through Matthew to start fresh with the Gospel of Mark.

NOTES:

NOTES:

The Salvational Names of Jesus

A B C Plan for the Study

Study Verses:

"For I know that my redeemer liveth, and that he shall stand at the latter day upon the earth" (Job 19:25).

"Let the words of my mouth, and the meditation of my heart be acceptable in thy sight, O LORD, my strength and my redeemer" (Psalm 19:14).

Study Goals:

1. To help group members understand some of the names applied to Jesus in the context of His saving work.
2. To lead group members into a deeper appreciation of Christ as their Saviour.

Materials Needed:

1. Copies of *The Names of Jesus* by Elmer L. Towns.
2. One copy of the Study 5 Lesson Outline and Discussion Sheet for each group member.

Advance Preparation:

1. Contact the group member(s) presenting the book review and/or special report to remind them of their involvement in this week's session.
2. Replace some of the names of Jesus in your room with new names which tie in more closely with this week's theme: the salvational names of Jesus.
3. You will need a large chart or pad of paper and marker to list names of Jesus toward the end of this session.

Approach

1. Begin this session celebrating the salvation we have in Jesus. Choose several testimonial hymns from your church's hymnal

that describe salvation in a different context or from a different perspective. Then prepare a worship time by singing a verse from one of these hymns, then reading a verse from another hymn. Sing three hymns and read two hymns to begin this session.

2. Have two or three group members lead in prayer thanking God for salvation and asking Him to guide them in today's study of the salvational names of Jesus.

NOTES:

III Bible Exploration

STEP 1: *Book Review*

1. In session two, you assigned a group member to prepare a brief book review. Have him or her introduce the book chosen and share briefly about the book. Use the suggested book review outline form on Discussion Sheet 2 as a guide for presenting the book.
2. If there is significant interest in the book on the part of other group members, let the reviewer field two or three questions from his or her fellow group members before moving on.

STEP 2: *Special Report*

1. In session three, you assigned a group member to prepare a special report on the theme of this chapter. Have this group member share briefly his or her findings with the rest of the group. The reporter should include his or her favorite salvational name of Jesus and explain briefly the reasons for that choice.

STEP 3: *Discussion*

Use the following questions as a basis for your discussion of chapter five.

1. From what has Christ redeemed us? What was the payment or ransom?
2. Why was the name Saviour neglected by the apostles? How can we avoid taking this title and work of Christ for granted?
3. How should we feel and act in response to Jesus' work as the Lamb of God?
4. When Christ is called Propitiation, what has He accomplished? What influence should this have on our lives?
5. Why is Christ called the last Adam? How does the influence of the first and last Adam affect our lives?

NOTES:

STEP 4: *Review*

1. Present a review of chapter five using the following outline:
   - A. Redeemer
     1. Christ has purchased the sinner in the marketplace (Galatians 3:10).
     2. In paying the price for our redemption, Christ has bought us "out of the marketplace" of sin (Galatians 3:13).
     3. In redeeming us, Christ has set us free, liberating us from sin (Galatians 4:5).
   - B. Saviour
     1. We have been saved from the guilt and penalty of sin.
     2. We are being saved from the habit and dominion of sin.
     3. We shall be saved from the infirmities and curse of sin.
   - C. The Lamb of God
     1. Under the law, God required the sacrifice of a lamb for sin.
     2. In keeping with the terms of His law, God provided His perfect Lamb as the ultimate sacrifice for sin.
   - D. Propitiation
     1. As our Propitiation, Jesus is the basis of our salvation (Luke 18:13).
     2. Because God loved us in this way, we should also love one another (I John 4:10-11).
   - E. The Last Adam
     1. Adam, by disobedience, plunged this world into the slavery of sin.
     2. Jesus, by obedience, brought this world back to Himself.
   - F. The Author of Eternal Salvation
     1. Jesus is the cause of our salvation, but He is also salvation itself.
     2. As the Pioneer of our faith, Jesus leads us into our salvation.
   - G. Mediator
     1. Jesus is the Mediator between God and people (I Timothy 2:5).
     2. Jesus is the Mediator of the new and better covenant acting as a guarantor who secures what could not otherwise be obtained (Hebrews 8:6, 9:15).

III Conclusion

1. *Brainstorming*. Ask group members to think of as many titles of Christ as possible that relate to our salvation. List each name on a chart as they are suggested. Group members may

wish to complete the chart on Discussion Sheet 5 during the discussion period.

2. Ask group members to choose one of the names on the chart and explain briefly what that title suggests about salvation.
3. Conclude this session by leading the group in prayer, thanking God for the greatness of the salvation He has provided.
4. *Alternate Conclusion.* If your study group includes members who are not Christians, take time to explain briefly how they can experience the salvational names of Jesus in their own life. You may want to invite them to talk with you after the session if they are interested in receiving Jesus as their Saviour.

Assignments:

1. Members prepare for the next study by reading chapter six in *The Names of Jesus.*
2. Contact the group member(s) presenting the book report and/ or special report next week to remind them of their involvement in the lesson.
3. You may want to enlist a couple of group members to help you with room decorations as you prepare for next week's session. Make your meeting area look like Christmas as you consider together the birth names of Jesus.
4. Encourage group members to continue their Bible reading and personal journal.

NOTES:

NOTES:

The Birth Names of Christ

A B C Plan for the Study

Study Verses:

"Therefore the Lord himself shall give you a sign: Behold, a virgin shall conceive, and bear a son, and shall call his name Immanuel" (Isaiah 7:14).

"For unto us a child is born, unto us a son is given: and the government shall be upon his shoulder: and his name shall be called Wonderful, Counsellor, The Mighty God, The Everlasting Father, The Prince of Peace" (Isaiah 9:6).

Study Goals:

1. To help group members understand the meaning of several names associated with the birth of Jesus.
2. To help group members grow in their appreciation of who Jesus was in His birth.
3. If you plan to have background Christmas music playing as group members arrive, be sure you have the necessary sound equipment to play your tapes, records or compact discs.

Materials Needed:

1. Copies of *The Names of Jesus* by Elmer L. Towns.
2. One copy of the Study 6 Lesson Outline and Discussion Sheet for each group member.

Advance Preparation:

1. Contact the group member(s) presenting the book review and/or special report to remind them of their involvement in this week's session.
2. Replace some of the names of Jesus in your room with new names which tie in more closely with this week's theme: the birth names of Jesus.
3. Decorate your meeting area to look like Christmas. You may wish to consider decorating a tree, hanging a wreath, or using other seasonal decorations to remind group members of the Christmas season.

Approach

1. As part of your Christmas theme, you may wish to have Christmas background music playing as group members arrive.
2. Distribute a copy of Study 6 Lesson Outline and Discussion Sheet to each group member as they arrive.
3. Begin this session by having group members share warm Christmas memories. Have each one begin with the line, "*The thing I like most about Christmas is . . .*"
4. Explain that Jesus *is* the reason for the season. Just as the family of a new baby is proud of its name and often has special reasons for choosing that name, so God is proud of several names associated with the incarnation of His Son. The purpose of this session is to look at some of the birth names of Jesus.

Bible Exploration

STEP 1: *Book Review*

1. In session two, you assigned a group member to prepare a brief book review. Have him or her introduce the book chosen and share briefly about the book. Use the suggested book review outline form as a guide for presenting the book.
2. If there is significant interest in the book on the part of other group members, let the reviewer field two or three questions from his or her fellow group members before moving on.

STEP 2: *Special Report*

1. In session three, you assigned a group member to prepare a special report on the theme of this chapter. Have this group member share briefly his or her findings. The reporter should include his or her favorite birth name of Jesus and explain briefly the reasons for that choice. Encourage participation from others in the group by referring to the chart on Discussion Sheet 6.

STEP 3: *Discussion*

Use the following questions as a basis for your discussion of chapter six.

1. Of all the individuals in Scripture with supernatural births, why is the birth of Christ the greatest?
2. How is Christ our Dayspring?
3. How should the name and work of Christ as Immanuel affect our daily lives?

NOTES:

NOTES:

4. Name several ways Christians may express their worship of our "Wonderful" Christ. What does the word "wonderful" really mean?
5. How and when does Christ counsel the believer?
6. Is Jesus the Prince of Peace today, or is this a future event?

STEP 4: *Review*

1. Present a review of chapter six using the following outline:
   - A. The Dayspring from on High
     1. The Revelation of Our Sin
     2. The Revitalization of Our Sorrow
     3. The Redirection of Our Steps
     4. The Redemption of Our Souls
   - B. Immanuel/Emmanuel
     1. The Effect of Immanuel
     2. The Experience of Immanuel
   - C. Wonderful
     1. A Definition of His Wonder
     2. A Recognition of His Wonder
     3. A Response to His Wonder
   - D. Counsellor
     1. The Qualification of the Counsellor
     2. The Character of His Counsel
     3. The Discerning of His Counsel
   - E. The Mighty God
   - F. The Everlasting Father
   - G. The Prince of Peace
2. Ask group members what name they would have chosen had they been asked to name that baby. Encourage them to share briefly their reasons for choosing that name.
3. Explain that although these names are related to His birth, they have relevance to our Christian life today. Ask, "How will the birth name you chose impact your life this week?"

III Conclusion

1. This lesson has looked at a number of names of Jesus suggested in the context of His birth. Ask group members what name they would have chosen had they been asked to name that baby. Encourage them to share briefly their reasons for choosing that name.

2. Although Christmas comes only once a year, Jesus still has the names given Him at His birth. Ask group members how the birth name they chose can impact the way they live for and relate to Christ this week.
3. Conclude your time together this week by singing a verse of a Christmas carol such as *O Come All Ye Faithful*.

NOTES:

Assignments:

1. Members prepare for the next study by reading chapter 7 in *The Names of Jesus.*
2. Contact the group member(s) presenting the book report and/ or special report next week to remind them of their involvement in the lesson.
3. Encourage group members to continue their Bible reading and journaling.

NOTES:

The Service Names of Christ

A B C Plan for the Study

Study Verse:

"Even as the Son of man came not to be ministered unto, but to minister, and to give his life a ransom for many" (Matthew 20:28; Mark 10:45).

Study Goals:

1. To help group members better understand the servant nature of Christ.
2. To lead group members to become actively involved in meaningful Christian service.

Materials Needed:

1. Copies of *The Names of Jesus* by Elmer L. Towns.
2. One copy of the Study 7 Lesson Outline and Discussion Sheet for each group member.

Advance Preparation:

1. Contact the group member(s) presenting the book review and/ or special report to remind them of their involvement in this week's session.
2. Replace some of the names of Jesus in your room with new names which tie in more closely with this week's theme: the service names of Jesus.
3. Talk with your pastor or another church leader to get several ideas of ministry projects which your group could undertake during the remaining weeks of this study series. Choose two or three you think would have strong appeal to your group members and leave the final choice of a specific project to the group.
4. You will need a note pad and marker to list problems during the brainstorming activity in this session.

Approach

1. Distribute a copy of Study 7 Lesson Outline and Discussion Sheet to each group member as they arrive.
2. Take a few minutes at the beginning of this session to brainstorm about common problems people have. Write each problem on the note pad as they are mentioned.
3. As a group, survey your list of problems and suggest a specific name of Jesus which speaks directly to that problem. Explain that there is a sense in which every name of Jesus is a service name, but there are some names which are especially significant in this context.

Bible Exploration

STEP 1: *Book Review*

1. In session two, you assigned a group member to prepare a brief book review. Have him or her introduce the book chosen and share briefly about the book. Use the suggested book review outline form as a guide for presenting the book.
2. If there is significant interest in the book on the part of other group members, let the reviewer field two or three questions from group members before moving on.

STEP 2: *Special Report*

1. In session three, you assigned a group member to prepare a special report on the theme of this chapter. Have this group member share briefly his or her findings with the rest of the group. The reporter should include his or her favorite service name of Jesus and explain briefly the reasons for that choice.

STEP 3: *Discussion*

Use the following questions as a basis for your discussion of chapter seven.

1. The service names of Christ which relate to His act of creation are Creator and Sustainer. Discuss each of these roles.
2. What are Christ's instructive names? What can we learn about Christ from each?
3. The sovereign names of Christ describe His role in giving direction to the believer. What can we learn about Christ from each of these names?
4. The assistance names of Christ reveal how Christ supports and helps the believer. Discuss the meaning and work involved in these names.

NOTES:

NOTES:

5. Share your reaction to reviewing these service names of Christ. Which is most meaningful to you? Why?

STEP 4: *Review*

1. Present a review of the seventh chapter using the following outline:
   A. The Creative Names of Jesus
   Read Colossians 1:16-17 to the group.
   B. The Instructive Names of Jesus
      1. *Rabbi* emphasizes the nature or content of Jesus' teaching.
      2. *Rabboni* identifies the relationship between Jesus the Teacher and we the learners.
      3. *Didaskalos* identifies the ongoing teaching ministry of Jesus.
      4. *Kathegetes* portrays the teaching of Jesus as a guide to life.
   C. The Sovereign Names of Jesus
      1. *Epistates* emphasizes Jesus' role in our life as overseer.
      2. *Oikodespotes* emphasizes Jesus' role as master over the household of faith.
      3. *Despostes* emphasizes the absolute ownership and power of Jesus over us.
   D. The Assistance Names of Jesus
      1. Jesus assists us through His ministry of intercession.
      2. Jesus assists us through His ministry of advocacy.
      3. As the Propitiation for our sins, Jesus paid a price that we could not pay ourselves.
      4. One of the means by which Jesus helps us live the Christian life is through His indwelling presence.
2. Present two or three ministry projects which could be done by your group and encourage the group to adopt one. These projects should be the kind which (1) do not necessarily involve an extended time commitment (i.e. no longer than a one month commitment), (2) appeal to the interest of group members, and (3) could be done well by people with the kind of gift mix represented in your group.

III Conclusion

1. ***Ministry Project.*** Just as Jesus committed His life to ministry, so we should also be involved in helping others. Present two or three ministry projects which could be done by your group and encourage the group to adopt one. These projects should be the kind which do not necessarily involve an extended time

commitment (i.e. no longer than a one month commitment), appeal to the interest of group members, and could be done well by people with the kind of gift mix represented in your group.

2. Appoint a ministry coordinator from the group who can work out the details associated with the project you choose and contact group members about their individual involvement.
3. Conclude this session with special prayer for the project your group has adopted.

Assignments:

1. Members prepare for the next study by reading chapter eight in *The Names of Jesus.*
2. Contact the group member(s) presenting the book report and/or special report next week to remind them of their involvement in the lesson.
3. This week group members will begin reading the Gospel of Luke. Once again, this is a good time for group members who have not kept up their journal to start doing so.

NOTES:

NOTES:

The Sonship Names of Christ

A B C Plan for the Study

Study Verse:

"I will declare the decree: the LORD hath said unto me, Thou art my Son; this day have I begotten thee" (Psalm 2:7).

Study Goals:

1. To help group members understand the meaning of three primary sonship names of Jesus.
2. To lead group members into a deeper appreciation of the uniqueness of Jesus.

Materials Needed:

1. Copies of *The Names of Jesus* by Elmer L. Towns.
2. One copy of the Study 8 Lesson Outline and Discussion Sheet for each group member.

Advance Preparation:

1. Contact the group member(s) presenting the book review and/ or special report to remind them of their involvement in this week's session.
2. Replace some of the names of Jesus in your room with new names which tie in more closely with this week's theme: the sonship names of Jesus.
3. Prepare a wall mural using pictures of men and boys together. Cut large construction paper letters to write the statement *Like Father Like Son* across the wall. Place it on the first wall group members are likely to notice as they enter the room.
4. Plug in the coffee pot early so fresh coffee is ready as the first group member arrives (or hot water for tea).

Approach

1. Sometimes it's good to take time to get to know one another a little better. Use coffee and an informal approach to greeting

people as they arrive for this study session to help establish a family atmosphere in the group if you do not already have one.

2. Begin by drawing attention to the motto *Like Father Like Son.* Explain that the family is the basic social unit in our society so it is not surprising that children pick up certain habits and life patterns from their parents. Invite group members to share their answers to the following questions: (1) *What is there of my parents that people notice in my life?* and (2) *What is there of me that I notice in the life of my children?*
3. Explain that the Hebrews used the expression "son of" to make comparisons of two people who were very similar. While there are 19 sonship names of Jesus in Scripture, this session will focus on the three most significant.
4. Distribute copies of the Study 8 Lesson Outline and Discussion Sheet to group members. Suggest that the students complete the chart as the discussion progresses.

III Bible Exploration

Step 1: *Book Review*

1. In session two, you assigned a group member to prepare a brief book review. Have him or her introduce the book chosen and share briefly about the book. (Use the suggested book review outline on Discussion Sheet 2.)
2. If there is significant interest in the book on the part of other group members, let the reviewer field two or three questions from his or her fellow group members before moving on.

Step 2: *Special Report*

1. In session three, you assigned a group member to prepare a special report on the theme of this chapter. Have this group member share briefly his or her findings with the rest of the group. The reporter should include his or her favorite sonship name of Jesus and explain briefly the reasons for that choice.

Step 3: *Discussion*

Use the following questions as a basis for your discussion of chapter eight.

1. Giving Jesus the title Son implies that the first Person of the Trinity is the Father. What do the sonship names reveal about the Trinity?
2. There are 19 sonship titles of Christ. Which three are predominant? Why? (See pages 94-99 of *The Names of Jesus.*)

NOTES:

NOTES:

3. Of all His names, which one did Christ use most frequently in reference to Himself? Why do you think He preferred this name?
4. Why was Jesus called the only begotten Son?
5. The title Son of God reminds us of the deity of Christ. Can a person be saved apart from belief in Christ's deity? Why or why not?

STEP 4: *Review*

1. Present a review of chapter eight using the following outline:
   - A. Son of Man
     1. This was the name Jesus used most often of Himself (over 80 times).
     2. Jesus was the Son of Man in the context of His earthly ministry.
     3. Jesus was the Son of Man in the context of His atoning death.
     4. Jesus is the Son of Man in an eschatological context.
   - B. The Only Begotten Son
     1. The Church Fathers coined the phrase "eternal generation" to express the idea that Jesus was eternally the Son of God, i.e. did not at some point become the Son of God.
     2. The word "begotten" emphasizes the uniqueness of Jesus.
   - C. The Son of God
     1. Jesus identified Himself as the Son of God.
     2. Jesus was identified as the Son of God by God the Father.
     3. The title Son of God does not imply Jesus is anything less than God the Son.

III Conclusion

1. Conclude this lesson as you began, by drawing attention to the statement *Like Father Like Son*. Apply this to your understanding of the character of Jesus. Ask, what do we know about God that must also be true of Jesus?
2. As adopted children of the Father, how does this statement apply to us?
3. If simply gaining a deeper understanding of who Jesus is is the only result of this study series, then we are missing the whole point of God revealing His Son through the many names of Jesus. Ask: How should we respond to Jesus in light of His sonship names?

4. Break up into prayer partners. Have group members share a specific prayer request coming out of his or her response to the above question, then have prayer partners pray for each other remembering that request.

Assignments:

1. Members prepare for the next study by reading chapter nine in *The Names of Jesus.*
2. Contact the group member(s) presenting the book report and/ or special report next week to remind them of their involvement in the lesson.
3. Encourage group members to continue reading the chapters of Luke listed on today's Discussion Sheet and make personal journal entries of insights regarding the names of Christ.

NOTES:

NOTES:

The Godhead Names of Christ

A B C Plan for the Study

Study Verse:

"And Simon Peter answered and said, Thou art the Christ, the Son of the living God" (Matthew 16:16).

Study Goals:

1. To lead group members to a deeper appreciation of Jesus as God.
2. To lead group members to respond in worship and obedience to the Godhead names of Christ.

Materials Needed:

1. Copies of *The Names of Jesus* by Elmer L. Towns.
2. One copy of the Study 9 Lesson Outline and Discussion Sheet for each group member.

Advance Preparation:

1. Contact the group member(s) presenting the book review and/ or special report to remind them of their involvement in this week's session.
2. Replace some of the names of Jesus in your room with new names which tie in more closely with this week's theme: the Godhead names of Jesus.
3. Prepare a list of the attributes of God and post it in a prominent place in your meeting area. Next to each attribute, write a reference to a verse that ascribes that attribute to Jesus. Page 106 in *The Names of Jesus* will be helpful in preparing the list.

Approach

1. Distribute a copy of the Study 9 Lesson Outline and Discussion Sheet to each group member as he or she arrives.
2. Draw attention to the chart of the attributes of God. Explain that an attribute of God is something which is true only about God.

3. Have different group members read the verses which ascribe these attributes to Jesus.
4. Explain that although the deity of Christ can be demonstrated by a comparison of divine attributes, Scripture also teaches this truth by calling Jesus God. This session will focus on the Godhead names of Christ.

NOTES:

III Bible Exploration

STEP 1: *Book Review*

1. In session two, you assigned a group member to prepare a brief book review. Have him or her introduce the book chosen and share briefly about the book. (Use the suggested book review outline form as a guide for presenting the book.)
2. If there is significant interest in the book on the part of other group members, let the reviewer field two or three questions from his or her fellow group members before moving on.

STEP 2: *Special Report*

1. In session three, you assigned a group member to prepare a special report on the theme of this chapter. Have this group member share briefly his or her findings with the rest of the group. The reporter should include his or her favorite Godhead name of Jesus and explain briefly the reasons for that choice.

STEP 3: *Discussion*

Use the following questions as a basis for your discussion of chapter nine.

1. Why is Jesus called the Word? What does this indicate about His character and work?
2. What does "accepted in the beloved" (Ephesians 1:6) mean?
3. As the Image of God, what does Christ reflect? How does this name relate to believers?
4. There are several names of Christ which come from the attributes of God. Discuss how each of these names reflects a different aspect of God's nature.
5. Does the title Firstborn imply that Christ came into existence at a point in time? Why or why not?
6. As the Passover, what does Christ do for the believer?
7. Christ is the Alpha and Omega. He is the beginning and ending of what? In light of this truth, how should we view our trials and struggles?

NOTES:

STEP 4: *Review*

Present a review of this passage using the following outline:

1. One of the key passages to understanding the deity of Christ is John 1:1-18 where Jesus is described as "the Word" (*Logos*).
   A. The phrase "In the beginning" is not a reference to a point in time but a reference to eternity past (1:1).
   B. The personality of the Word is evident in that it is capable of individualization (1:1).
   C. The Word has active and personal communication with God (1:1-2).
   D. There are two centers of Consciousness, for the Word was God yet also "face to face" or "with" God (1:1).
   E. The Word has the essence of deity (1:1).
   F. The Father and the Word are one (1:1).
   G. The Word was the Agent by which God expressed or revealed Himself (1:18).
   H. The incarnate Word has a definite continuity with the preincarnate Word (1:1, 14).
   I. As God lived in a tent, spoke in a tent, and revealed Himself in the Old Testament tabernacle, so the Word tabernacled among us (1:14).
   J. The incarnation of the Word is the unique revelation of God (1:14).
2. The Godhead of Christ is also emphasized in the attributive names of Jesus. Read those names identified on page 106 or compose your own list of Jesus' names which draw attention to His possessing the attributes of God.
3. A third group of names emphasizing the deity of Christ are His priority names. Review the emphasis of those names listed on pages 107 and 108.

III Conclusion

1. One of the best responses to the Godhead names of Jesus is to worship Jesus as God. Encourage group members to share a Scripture or verse of a hymn that draws attention to the deity of Christ.
2. After a brief time of worship using Scripture and song, have several group members lead the group in prayer. Sometimes it is easy to take God for granted. As you close in prayer, pray that each group member would consciously respond to Jesus as God throughout this week. You might also choose to close by singing one of the hymns as a benediction and commission for the coming week.

Assignments:

1. Members prepare for the next study by reading chapter ten in *The Names of Jesus.*
2. Contact the group member(s) presenting the book report and/or special report next week to remind them of their involvement in the lesson.
3. Remind group members they will be sharing from their journal in session twelve. Ask them to begin thinking of which name has made the deepest impression on them during this study series.

NOTES:

NOTES:

The Jehovistic Titles of Christ

A B C Plan for the Study

Study Verse:

"Jesus said unto them, Verily, verily, I say unto you, Before Abraham was, I am" (John 8:58).

Study Goals:

1. To lead group members to know the "I am" titles of Christ in the Gospel of John.
2. To help group members allow Jesus "to become" Jehovah in their Christian experience.

Materials Needed:

1. Copies of *The Names of Jesus* by Elmer L. Towns.
2. One copy of the Study 10 Lesson Outline and Discussion Sheet for each group member.
3. You will need the items which symbolize the "I am" statements around which this session is based. (See note below on room decoration.)

Advance Preparation:

1. Contact the group member(s) presenting the book review and/ or special report to remind them of their involvement in this week's session.
2. *Room Decoration.* This week, remove the names of Jesus from the wall and use the "I am" statements as a basis for your meeting area's decoration. Include items such as a loaf of bread or a basket of rolls (Bread of Life), a lamp or candle (Light of the World), a bowl of grapes (True Vine), etc. Throughout this session, draw attention to these items as you discuss these names.

Approach

1. Distribute a copy of Study 10 Lesson Outline and Discussion Sheet to each group member as he or she arrives.

2. As you begin this session, have group members describe something about themselves using a comparison. Begin with the statement, "*If I were an animal, I would be a. . . .*" Then ask each group member to explain the reason for his or her choice of an animal.
3. Explain that people commonly use comparisons to communicate a likeness to others. On several occasions, Jesus also used comparisons to identify something about Himself. This session will look at the "I am" statements in John.

NOTES:

III Bible Exploration

STEP 1: *Book Review*

1. In session two, you assigned a group member to prepare a brief book review. Have him or her introduce the book chosen and share briefly about the book. (The suggested book review outline form is on Discussion Sheet 2.)
2. If there is significant interest in the book on the part of other group members, let the reviewer field two or three questions from group members before moving on.

STEP 2: *Special Report*

1. In session three, you assigned a group member to prepare a special report on the theme of this chapter. Have this group member share briefly his or her findings with the rest of the group. The reporter should include his or her favorite "I am" name of Jesus and explain briefly the reasons for that choice.

STEP 3: *Discussion*

Use the following questions as a basis for your discussion of chapter ten.

1. What is important about the I AMs of the eight Jehovistic titles of Christ? How do they reflect His deity?
2. What is the purpose of bread? How does Christ fulfill this purpose for believers?
3. What did Christ mean when He described Himself as light?
4. Relate the function of a door to Christ's ministry. What does it mean to go in and out?
5. How is Christ a Good Shepherd?
6. What twofold promise is extended because of Christ's title of Resurrection and Life?
7. When Christ said, "I am. . .I am," what did He imply? What do we know about Christ because of these Jehovistic titles?

NOTES:

STEP 4: *Review*

1. Present a review of chapter ten using the following outline:
   - A. I am the Bread of Life
     1. The Jews believed their Messiah would produce the jar of manna hidden in the ark as a sign of who He was.
     2. Jesus is the fulfillment of the type of the Hidden Manna.
     3. As the Bread of Life, Jesus is the nourishment we need in our Christian life.
   - B. I am the Light of the World
     1. As the Light of the World, Jesus reveals Himself, the Father and the cross.
     2. He is the Light of the World in the sense of being the light energy itself.
     3. We are the lights of the world in the sense of being the lamps through which the light shines.
   - C. I am the Door
     1. Jesus is the Door to salvation.
     2. Jesus is also the Door to Christian service.
   - D. I am the Good Shepherd
     1. Our Good Shepherd is deeply concerned for and cares for His sheep.
     2. As Christians, we also have a shepherding responsibility in caring for one another.
   - E. I am the Resurrection and the Life
     1. This name carries the promise of the resurrection of the saints.
     2. This name carries the promise of exemption from the second death.
   - F. I am the Way, the Truth, and the Life
     1. Jesus is the exclusive way to God.
     2. Jesus is the embodiment of all truth.
     3. Jesus is also the embodiment of all life.
   - G. I am the True Vine
     1. While Israel is compared to a vine, it has become a wild vine which fails to produce fruit.
     2. Jesus described Himself as the true (genuine) vine.
   - H. I am. . .I am
     1. On a few occasions, Jesus used the title "I am" independent of a further description.
     2. The title "I am" is the root of the Old Testament name of God, *Jehovah*.

III Conclusion

1. Share G. Campbell Morgan's suggestion that the name Jehovah could be better experienced if it were translated "to become."
2. Encourage two or three group members to share a personal experience in which Jesus became real to them in the context of one of these Jehovistic names.
3. Close this session in prayer asking God to bring experiences into the lives of each group member this week that will help them come to know Jesus in the context of one of these Jehovistic names.

Assignments:

1. Members prepare for the next study by reading chapter eleven in *The Names of Jesus.*
2. Contact the group member(s) presenting the book report and/or special report next week to remind them of their involvement in the lesson.
3. This week group members will complete the book of Luke and should begin reading John as the basis of their journaling.

NOTES:

NOTES:

The Church Names of Christ

A B C Plan for the Study

Study Verse:

"And I say also unto thee, That thou art Peter, and upon this rock I will build my church; and the gates of hell shall not prevail against it" (Matthew 16:18).

Study Goals:

1. To help group members better understand the relationship of Christ to His church.
2. To lead group members to become actively involved in the ministry of their local church.

Materials Needed:

1. Copies of *The Names of Jesus* by Elmer L. Towns.
2. One copy of the Study 11 Lesson Outline and Discussion Sheet for each group member.

Advance Preparation:

1. Contact the group member(s) presenting the book review and/ or special report to remind them of their involvement in this week's session.
2. Use pictures of your church and/or various church activities to decorate your room this week.
3. Contact your pastor or other church leader for information about ministries presently looking for workers. Obtain job descriptions for those ministry openings which would be best suited for people with the gifts of your group members.
4. If your group is involved in the process of choosing your study theme, visit your Christian bookstore this week and obtain consignment copies of several possible study books for your next study series.

Approach

1. Begin this session by asking group members to complete the

following statements: (1) *When I think of the church, I think of a....* (2) *When I think of Jesus and the church, I think of....*

2. Distribute a copy of Study 11 Lesson Outline and Discussion Sheet to each group member.
3. Explain that Jesus used several pictures of the church to describe His relationship to the church. This session will look at five of those pictures.

NOTES:

III Bible Exploration

STEP 1: *Book Review*

1. In session two, you assigned a group member to prepare a brief book review. Have him or her introduce the book chosen and share briefly about the book. The suggested book review outline form gives a guide for presenting the book.
2. If there is significant interest in the book on the part of other group members, let the reviewer field two or three questions from group members before moving on.

STEP 2: *Special Report*

1. In session three, you assigned a group member to prepare a special report on the theme of this chapter. Have this group member share briefly his or her findings with the rest of the group. The reporter should include his or her favorite church name of Jesus and explain briefly the reasons for that choice.

STEP 3: *Discussion*

Use the following questions as a basis for your discussion of chapter eleven in *The Names of Jesus*.

1. Discuss the five titles for Christ mentioned in this chapter. What unique ministry is highlighted in each title?
2. How can we express our submission to Christ as the Head of the Body?
3. Discuss how Jesus the Shepherd is the model for pastors in caring for the flock.
4. As a Bridegroom, what does Christ do for those who are His bride?
5. List several contributions that a foundation makes to a building. How do these relate to the believer's life and his cornerstone, Christ?
6. Why does Jesus add the qualifying term "true" when He calls Himself a vine? How does Christ the Vine relate to believers as branches?

NOTES:

Conclusion

1. Have someone read Ephesians 5:25. Explain that if Jesus loved the church enough to die for it, we ought to love our church enough to serve in it.
2. Report on your conversation with your pastor or other church leader about present ministry opportunities. Share briefly the character of each job and the spiritual gifts which are most likely to be used.
3. Have copies of each job description available to group members. Include the name and phone number of the person to be contacted if group members are interested in pursuing that opportunity.
4. As you conclude in prayer, have special prayer for the ministries in which group members are already serving and the need for additional workers.
5. If your group is involved in the process of choosing topics for your Bible study, take a few moments at the conclusion of this session to review the books you obtained at the bookstore and choose your next study book.

Assignments:

1. Members prepare for the next study by reading chapter 12 in *The Names of Jesus.*
2. Contact the group member(s) presenting the book report and/ or special report next week to remind them of their involvement in the lesson.
3. Remind each group member he or she will be given an opportunity to share the most significant lesson learned in his or her personal study of the names of Jesus. Encourage them to review their journal this week in preparation for next week's session.
4. Decide what Bible study will be the basis of your next study series and order enough copies for each group member. Distribute them next week.

NOTES:

The Apocalyptic Names of Christ

A B C Plan for the Study

Study Verse:

"The Revelation of Jesus Christ, which God gave unto him, to shew unto his servants things which must shortly come to pass; and he sent and signified it by his angel unto his servant John" (Revelation 1:1).

Study Goals:

1. To lead group members to understand and appreciate the names by which Jesus has revealed Himself to them.
2. To encourage group members to grow in their relationship with Jesus and share that growth with others.

Materials Needed:

1. Copies of *The Names of Jesus* by Elmer L. Towns.
2. One copy of the Study 12 Lesson Outline and Discussion Sheet for each group member.
3. Copies of the study book which will serve as the basis for your next study series.

Advance Preparation:

1. Contact the group member(s) presenting the book review and/ or special report to remind them of their involvement in this week's session.
2. Call group members a few days before the meeting to remind them of the opportunity to share the most significant lesson they have learned in this study of the names of Jesus. Encourage them to review their journal to see what the Lord has been teaching them.
3. Write the 72 names and titles of Christ which occur in the Revelation on pieces of paper. Prior to the beginning of this week's session, hide the names around the room.
4. Pick up the next study books from the bookstore to be distributed to group members at the conclusion of this session.

NOTES:

■ Approach

1. *Find the Names.* As group members arrive, tell them there are 72 names and titles of Christ hidden in the room. Ask them to find and collect as many names as possible before the meeting begins.
2. Begin this session by having group members read the names they have found. If some have not been found, show the group where they were hidden and read those names also.
3. Explain that God hid many things about Jesus early in the Scripture but the fullest revelation of who Jesus is is found in the book of Revelation.
4. Distribute a copy of Study 12 Lesson Outline and Discussion Sheet to each group member.

■ Bible Exploration

STEP 1: *Book Review*

1. In session two, you assigned a group member to prepare a brief book review. Have him or her introduce the book chosen and share briefly about the book. Use the suggested book review outline form as a guide for presenting the book.
2. If there is significant interest in the book on the part of other group members, let the reviewer field two or three questions from group members before moving on.

STEP 2: *Special Report*

1. In session three, you assigned a group member to prepare a special report on the theme of this chapter. Have this group member share briefly his or her findings with the rest of the group. The reporter should include his or her favorite apocalyptic name of Jesus and explain briefly the reasons for that choice.

STEP 3: *Discussion*

Use the following questions as a basis for your discussion of chapter twelve.

1. Why does the last book in the Bible, Revelation, have perhaps more names of Jesus than any other? What is the main theme of this book?
2. Why is Revelation called a climactic book?
3. What is the threefold picture of Jesus in Revelation? Relate it to His threefold anointed offices.

4. Note the contrasting descriptions of Christ as a Lion and Lamb. How do these titles carry out the theme of Revelation? What do these titles tell us about Christ?
5. Name the titles in Revelation that describe Christ as a conqueror. What do these titles tell us about Christ?
6. Explain how Christ is the Root and Offspring of David.

NOTES:

STEP 4: *Review*

Present a review of this chapter using the following outline:

Dr. Towns writes, *John was a climactic writer. . . .Climactically, he wrote the last of the four Gospels. Climactically, he was the last person to write Scripture. Climactically, his Gospel is the greatest thesis on Christ. Climactically, his book was the last to be recognized as cannonical. Climactically, he wrote the last book of the Bible. Climatically, he wrote concerning the last things.* Explain that it is fitting that this last lesson in our study series should focus on the names of Jesus in the climactic book of Revelation.

1. Jesus Christ
   A. As our Prophet, Jesus is the Faithful Witness.
   B. As our Priest, Jesus is the First Begotten of the Dead.
   C. As our King, Jesus is the Prince of the Kings of the Earth.
2. His Eternal Completeness and Sufficiency
   A. Jesus is the Alpha and Omega, everything from A to Z.
   B. Jesus is the Beginning and Ending.
   C. Jesus is the Lord who was, is and is to come.
   D. Jesus is the Almighty.
3. The Son of Man
   A. John saw Jesus as the Son of Man in the midst of the churches.
   B. As the Son of Man, Jesus was exactly what the churches needed.
   C. If people are going to see Jesus today, they will also see Him in the midst of the churches.
4. The Lion and the Lamb
5. The Coming Conqueror
   A. The Conqueror is described by the name Faithful and True.
   B. There is at least one name of Jesus which no one knows.
   C. Jesus conquers by His name—the Word of God.
   D. Ultimately, Jesus is the King of Kings and Lord of Lords.
6. The Root and Offspring of David
7. The Bright and Morning Star

NOTES:

III Conclusion

1. Take time at the conclusion of this session to encourage group members to share briefly the most significant lesson learned during this study. Some group members may wish to read something from their journals which was written when this truth first became real to them.
2. During the past 12 sessions, your group has learned many new names of Jesus. Lead your group in a time of sentence prayers. Encourage group members to address Jesus by one of His many names and praise Him or ask Him for something relevant to that particular name (i.e. someone might thank the Shepherd for evidence of His care for them during the past week, or ask the Light of the World to help them see God's will in their present situation).
3. After all have had opportunity to be involved in prayer, lead your group in singing a popular hymn or chorus that celebrates the Name of Jesus. (Check your hymnbook for an appropriate hymn.)
4. Before group members leave, give each one: (1) A copy of today's Discussion Sheet which will take some time to prepare during the week. Urge them to complete "This Week in the Word" contained on the sheet and to take five more days to finish their reading of the Gospels. (2) Give them the next study book and next week's assignment.

Assignments:

1. During this study series, group members have been introduced to the discipline of journaling. Encourage group members to make journaling an ongoing spiritual discipline in their life.
2. Check your new leader's guide for specific group assignments for next week.

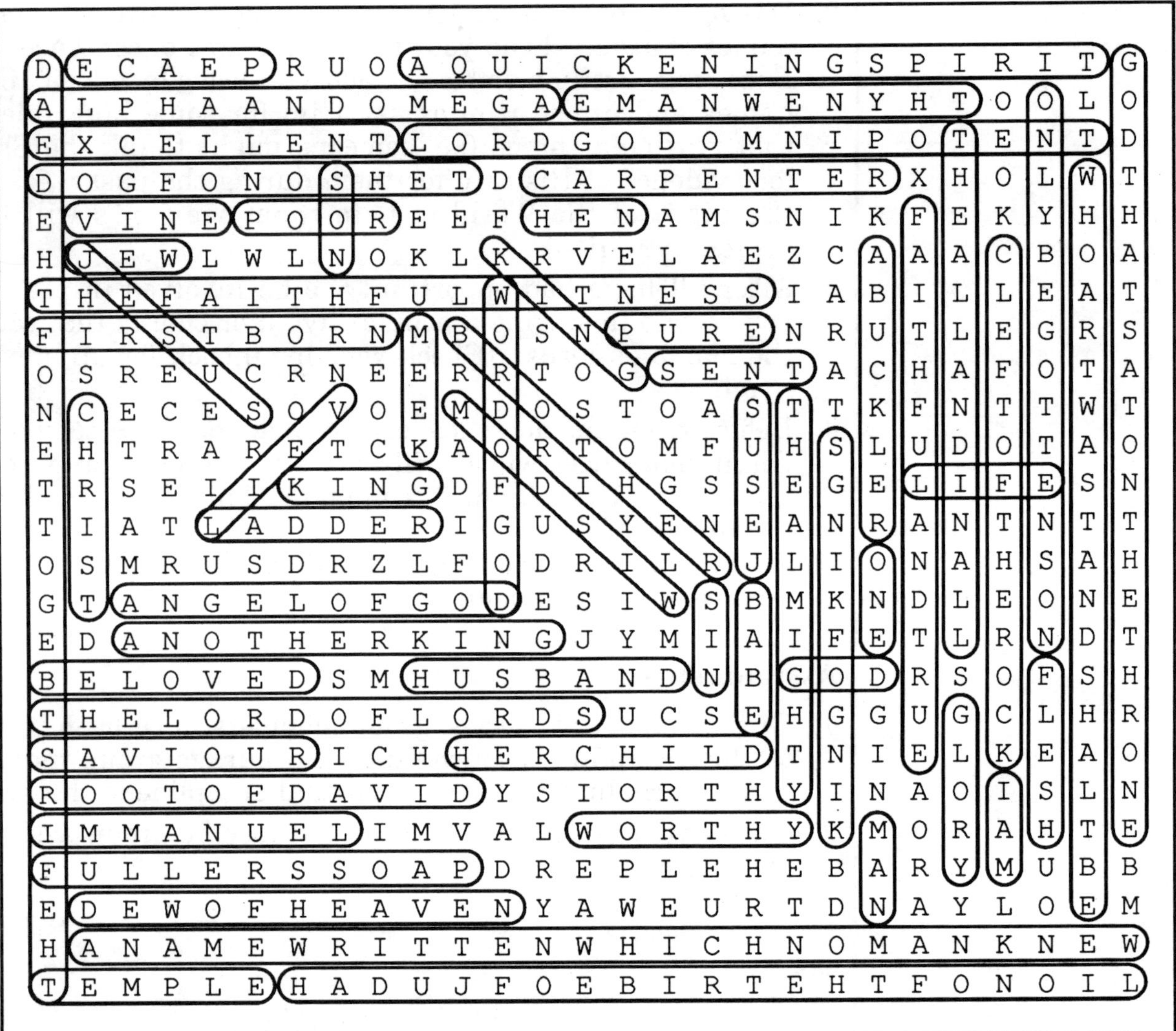

The Name of Jesus

"And she shall bring forth a son, and thou shalt call his name JESUS: for he shall save his people from their sins" (Matthew 1:21).

Lesson Notes:

A. The Meaning of His Identification
   1. The name Jesus/Joshua means "Jehovah the Saviour."
   2. When applied to Joshua in the Old Testament, it was an expression of faith in Jehovah's purpose to save His people.
   3. When applied to Jesus in the New Testament, it was an expression of the nature of Jesus. He was "Jehovah the Saviour."

B. The Mystery of His Incarnation
   1. Jesus was so named because He was *"God in the flesh."*
   2. The means by which God became a man involved the miracle of the virgin birth.

C. The Marvels of His Occupation
   1. As "Jehovah the Saviour," Jesus' primary work was the *saving* of His people from their sins.
   2. The extent of His saving work was first recognized by the Samaritans who identified Him as *"the Saviour of the World."*

D. The Majesty of His Reputation
   1. God has given Jesus "a name which is above every name."
   2. As Christians, we have a moral responsibility to "live up to the name of Jesus."
   3. In prayer, Christians should pray "in Jesus' name" which means to pray on the basis of *Jesus' merit* rather than their own.
   4. There is a *unique spiritual power* in the name of Jesus.
   5. The name of Jesus is a worthy object of our worship and meditation.

Study 2 Outline

The Title "Lord"

"For unto you is born this day in the city of David a Saviour, which is Christ the Lord" (Luke 2:11).

"Therefore let all the house of Israel know assuredly, that God hath made that same Jesus, whom ye crucified, both Lord and Christ" (Acts 2:36).

"That if thou shalt confess with thy mouth the Lord Jesus, and shalt believe in thine heart that God hath raised him from the dead, thou shalt be saved" (Romans 10:9).

Lesson Notes:

A. The Meaning of this Name

1. The Greek word *kurios*, translated "Lord," is used in the New Testament to describe an owner (Luke 19:33), one who has disposal of anything (Matthew 12:8), a master to whom service is due (Matthew 6:24), an emperor or king (Acts 25:26; Revelation 17:14), a father (Matthew 21:30), husband (I Peter 3:6), master (Matthew 13:27), ruler (Matthew 27:63), angel (Acts 10:4), a stranger (Acts 16:30), a pagan idol or deity (I Corinthians 8:5), and the Old Testament name of God (*Jehovah* - Matthew 4:7; *Adonai* - Matthew 1:22; *Elohim* - I Peter 1:25).
2. When this title is ascribed to Jesus, it recognizes His (a) right to *respect*, (b) right to *be served*, (c) right of *disposal*, and (d) right to *rule and hold authority over others.*
3. This title implies Jesus' *absolute control* in the lives of His disciples. Compare the contrast between the use of "Master" and "Lord" by Peter (Luke 5:5-8) and the disciples (Matthew 26:22-25).
4. Thomas used the expression *"my Lord and my God"* (John 20:28) to affirm His faith in Jesus. This was also the constant theme of apostolic preaching (II Corinthians 4:5).

B. The Message of This Name

1. The title "Lord" is closely related to what it means to be a Christian (Romans 10:9).
2. Recognizing the Lordship of Christ is a work of *the Holy Spirit* in our life (I Corinthians 12:3) which we need to recognize and apply personally (I Peter 3:15; Romans 12:1).
3. The essence of *Christian stewardship* is recognizing the Lordship of Christ over everything (Psalm 24:1).
4. Lordship means *"absolute surrender"* to the will of God.
5. Lordship is applied practically in our life in four steps.

a. *Knowing* the doctrinal basis of our victory in the Christian life, i.e. our union with Christ (Romans 6:3, 6, 9).
b. *Reckoning* or relying on that fact to be true in our experience (Romans 6:11).
c. *Yielding* to His Lordship "once and for all" (Romans 6:13, 16, 19).
d. *Obeying* Christ as an expression of our yieldedness to His will (Romans 6:16-17).

Study 3 Outline

The Office of Christ

"Come, see a man, which told me all things that ever I did: is not this the Christ?" (John 4:29).

Lesson Notes:

A. The Messiah in the Old Testament

1. Like Moses, the Messiah was viewed as an anointed *Prophet* (Deuteronomy 18:15-19). What makes a prophet a prophet? Prophets were called:
   a. *"The Man of God"* — emphasizing his relationship to God, his message from God, and his godly character.
   b. *"The Servant of God"* — expressing willingness to obey God and involvement in the ministry of prayer.
   c. *"The Prophet (Nabi')"* — which is derived from the verb "to call." The prophet was one who was called of God.
   d. *"The Seer (Ro'eh/Hozeh)"* — which stresses their vision.
   e. The Greek verb *prophaino* means "to reveal" and includes both predicting the future and revealing God's message.
   f. The Greek verb *prothemi* means "to tell forth" as one who declares God's message.
   g. The prophet was a "For-teller" *(Spokesman for God)*, "Foreteller" *(Predictor of future events)*, and "Forth-teller" *(Preacher to people)*.
2. Like Melchizedek, the Messiah was viewed as an anointed *Priest* (Psalm 110:4). What made a priest a priest?
   a. He was called of God to this ministry.
   b. He represented others before God.
   c. He offered the sacrifice for sin.
   d. He prayed on behalf of others (intercession).
3. Like David, the Messiah was viewed as an anointed *King* (II Samuel 16:13). How do we recognize the kingship of Jesus?
   a. His kingship is derived from His deity (I Timothy 1:17).
   b. As King, He has a kingdom (John 18:36).
   c. If Jesus is our King, we are His subjects (Luke 17:10).

B. The Christ in the New Testament

1. Although Jesus never used this title of Himself, He commended those who did (Matthew 16:16-17). It is most probable that those who used this expression in the Gospels and early chapters of Acts did so with the Old Testament anointed offices in mind.

2. One of the major themes in the writings of Paul is that of the union of Christ and the believer. He uses the expression "in Christ" 172 times to express this thought.
3. Our *union with Christ* refers to our non-experiential state or position in heaven as believers.
4. Our *communion with Christ* refers to our experiential realization of the intimate relationship we already have with Christ.

Study 4 Outline

The Old Testament Prophetic Names of Jesus

"And beginning at Moses and all the prophets, he expounded unto them, in all the scriptures the things concerning himself" (Luke 24:27).

Lesson Notes:

A. Shiloh means "peace maker" and refers to Jesus as the one who makes peace between God and humanity (Genesis 49:10; Isaiah 9:6).

B. Branch (*Netzer*)

1. This title may refer to the *negative reputation* Jesus bore based on His childhood home (Matthew 2:23; Isaiah 14:19).
2. The four Gospels emphasize four aspects of the Branch-character of Jesus (Matthew - *David* a righteous Branch [Jeremiah 23:5]; Mark - My *servant* the Branch [Zechariah 3:8]; Luke - the *man* whose name is the Branch [Zechariah 6:12]; John - the Branch of *the Lord* [Isaiah 4:2]).

C. Desire of All Nations

1. According to Jewish commentators, the second temple lacked five things: (a) the ark of the covenant with its mercy seat, (b) the tables of the law, (c) the holy fire, (d) the urim and thummim, and (e) the Shekinah glory of God.
2. As the Desire of All Nations, Jesus visited that temple. He was Himself (a) the propitiation for our sins (I John 2:2), (b) the Lawgiver (James 4:12), (c) the Wall of Fire (Zechariah 2:5), (d) the Urim and Thummim (Exodus 28:30), and (e) the Glory of the Father (John 1:14).

D. Ensign of the Peoples — the flag which brings all believers from all places together.

E. El Shaddai — The Almighty

1. *El Shaddai* describes *"the mother-love of God."*
2. *El Shaddai* has been translated *"The God who is Enough."*
3. *El Shaddai* was Job's favorite name for God implying God supplied what was needed to comfort Job's pain.

The Salvational Names of Jesus

"For I know that my redeemer liveth, and that he shall stand at the latter day upon the earth" (Job 19:25).

"Let the words of my mouth, and the meditation of my heart be acceptable in thy sight, O LORD, my strength and my redeemer" (Psalm 19:14).

Lesson Notes:

A. Redeemer
   1. Christ has purchased the sinner in the marketplace (Galatians 3:10).
   2. In paying the price for our redemption, Christ bought us "out of the marketplace" of sin (Galatians 3:13).
   3. In redeeming us, Christ set us free, liberating us from sin (Galatians 4:5).

B. Saviour
   1. We *have been saved* from the guilt and penalty of sin.
   2. We *are being saved* from the habit and dominion of sin.
   3. We *shall be saved* from the infirmities and curse of sin.

C. The Lamb of God
   1. Under the law, God required the sacrifice of a lamb for sin.
   2. In keeping with the terms of His law, God provided His perfect Lamb as the ultimate sacrifice for sin.

D. Propitiation
   1. As our Propitiation, Jesus is the basis of our salvation (Luke 18:13).
   2. Because God loved us in this way, we should also *love one another* (I John 4:10-11).

E. The Last Adam
   1. Adam, *by disobedience,* plunged this world into the slavery of sin.
   2. Jesus, *by obedience,* brought this world back to Himself.

F. The Author of Eternal Salvation
   1. Jesus is *the cause* of our salvation, but He is also salvation itself.
   2. As the Pioneer of our faith, Jesus *leads us into* our salvation.

G. Mediator
   1. Jesus is the Mediator between God and people (I Timothy 2:5).
   2. Jesus is the Mediator of the new and better covenant acting as a guarantor who secures what could not otherwise be obtained (Hebrews 8:6, 9:15).

Study 6 Outline

The Birth Names of Christ

"Therefore the Lord himself shall give you a sign: Behold, a virgin shall conceive, and bear a son, and shall call his name Immanuel" (Isaiah 7:14).

"For unto us a child is born, unto us a son is given: and the government shall be upon his shoulder: and his name shall be called Wonderful, Counsellor, The Mighty God, The Everlasting Father, The Prince of Peace" (Isaiah 9:6).

Lesson Notes:

A. The Dayspring from on High
   1. The *Revelation* of Our Sin
   2. The *Revitalization* of Our Sorrow
   3. The *Redirection* of Our Steps
   4. The *Redemption* of Our Souls

B. Immanuel/Emmanuel
   1. The *Effect* of Immanuel
   2. The *Experience* of Immanuel

C. Wonderful
   1. A *Definition* of His Wonder
   2. A *Recognition* of His Wonder
   3. A *Response* to His Wonder

D. Counsellor
   1. The *Qualification* of the Counsellor
   2. The *Character* of His Counsel
   3. The *Discerning* of His Counsel

E. The Mighty God

F. The Everlasting Father

G. The Prince of Peace

What name would you have given Jesus at His birth?

Study 7 Outline

The Service Names of Christ

"Even as the Son of man came not to be ministered unto, but to minister, and to give his life a ransom for many" (Matthew 20:28; Mark 10:45).

Lesson Notes:

A. The Creative Names of Jesus
   See Colossians 1:16-17

B. The Instructive Names of Jesus
   1. *Rabbi* emphasizes the *nature or content* of Jesus' teaching.
   2. *Rabboni* identifies the *relationship* between Jesus the Teacher and we the learners.
   3. *Didaskalos* identifies the *ongoing teaching* ministry of Jesus.
   4. *Kathegetes* portrays the teaching of Jesus as a *guide to life.*

C. The Sovereign Names of Jesus
   1. *Epistates* emphasizes Jesus' role in our life as *overseer.*
   2. *Oikodespotes* emphasizes Jesus' role as *master* over the household of faith.
   3. *Despotes* emphasizes the *absolute ownership* and power of Jesus over us.

D. The Assistance Names of Jesus
   1. Jesus assists us through His ministry of *intercession.*
   2. Jesus assists us through His ministry of *advocacy.*
   3. As the Propitiation for our sins, Jesus paid a price that we could not pay ourselves.
   4. One way Jesus helps us live the Christian life is through His indwelling presence.

I can model the service names of Christ through a ministry of:

Study 8 Outline

The Sonship Names of Jesus

"I will declare the decree: the LORD hath said unto me, Thou art my Son; this day have I begotten thee" (Psalm 2:7).

Lesson Notes:

A. Son of Man
   1. This was the name Jesus used most often of Himself (over 80 times).
   2. Jesus was the Son of Man in the context of His earthly ministry.
   3. Jesus was the Son of Man in the context of His atoning death.
   4. Jesus is the Son of Man in an eschatological context.

B. The Only Begotten Son
   1. The Church Fathers coined the phrase *"eternal generation"* to express the idea that Jesus was eternally the Son of God. (i.e. He did not at some point *become* the Son of God.)
   2. The word "begotten" emphasizes *the uniqueness of Jesus.*

C. The Son of God
   1. Jesus identified Himself as the Son of God.
   2. Jesus was identified as the Son of God by God the Father.
   3. The title Son of God does not imply Jesus is anything less than God the Son.

The Godhead Names of Christ

"And Simon Peter answered and said, Thou art the Christ, the Son of the living God" (Matthew 16:16).

Lesson Notes:

A. The Word (*Logos*)

1. The phrase *"In the beginning"* is not a reference to a point in time but a reference to eternity past (John 1:1).
2. The personality of the Word is evident in that it is capable of individualization (1:1).
3. The Word has active and personal *communication* with God (1:1-2).
4. There are two centers of Consciousness, for the Word was God yet also "face to face" or "with" God (1:1).
5. The Word has the *essence of deity* (1:1).
6. The Father and the Word are *one* (1:1).
7. The Word was the Agent by which God expressed or revealed Himself (John 1:18).
8. The incarnate Word has a definite continuity with the preincarnate Word (1:1, 14).
9. As God lived in a tent, spoke in a tent, and revealed Himself in the Old Testament tabernacle, so the Word tabernacled among us (1:14).
10. The Incarnation of the Word is the unique revelation of God (1:14).

B. The Attributive Names of Jesus (Page 106 of *The Names of Jesus*)

Name of Jesus	*Attribute of God*
______________	______________
______________	______________
______________	______________

C. The Priority Names of Jesus (Page 107 of *The Names of Jesus*)

____

____

____

Study 10 Outline

The Jehovistic Titles of Christ

"Jesus said unto them, Verily, verily, I say unto you, Before Abraham was, I am" (John 8:58).

Lesson Notes:

A. I am the Bread of Life (John 6:35)
   1. The Jews believed their Messiah would produce the jar of manna hidden in the ark as a sign of who He was.
   2. Jesus is the fulfillment of the type of the *Hidden Manna.*
   3. As the Bread of Life, Jesus is the nourishment we need in our Christian life.

B. I am the Light of the World (John 8:12)
   1. As the Light of the World, Jesus reveals Himself, the Father, and the cross.
   2. He is the Light of the World in the sense of being the light energy itself.
   3. We are the lights of the world in the sense of being the lamps through which the light shines.

C. I am the Door (John 10:9)
   1. Jesus is the Door to *salvation.*
   2. Jesus is also the Door to *Christian service.*

D. I am the Good Shepherd (John 10:11)
   1. Our Good Shepherd is deeply concerned about and cares for His sheep.
   2. As Christians, we also have a shepherding responsibility in caring for one another.

E. I am the Resurrection and the Life (John 11:25)
   1. This name carries the promise of the resurrection of the saints.
   2. This name carries the promise of exemption from the second death.

F. I am the Way, the Truth, and the Life (John 14:6)
   1. Jesus is the exclusive way to God.
   2. Jesus is the embodiment of all truth.
   3. Jesus is also the embodiment of all life.

G. I am the True Vine (John 15:1, 5)
   1. While Israel is compared to a vine, it has become a wild vine which fails to produce fruit.
   2. Jesus described Himself as the true (genuine) vine.

H. I AM. . .I AM (John 8:58, 18:5, 6, 8)

1. On a few occasions, Jesus used the title "I am" independent of a further description.
2. The title "I am" is the root of the Old Testament name of God *Jehovah*.

The Church Names of Christ

"And I say also unto thee, That thou art Peter, and upon this rock I will build my church; and the gates of hell shall not prevail against it" (Matthew 16:18).

When I think of the church, I think of a

When I think of Jesus and the church, I think of

Lesson Notes:

A. The Head of the Body

1. The body is the best known and most widely used symbol of the church in Scripture.
2. As the Head of the Body, Christ is the *determinative center* of the church which is His body.
3. This name implies that His purpose cannot be frustrated.
4. If Christ is the Head, no one else can claim preeminence in the church.
5. As members of the body, we need to yield to the Head.

B. The Shepherd of the Sheep

1. Jesus was the Good Shepherd in His death *(Psalm 22).*
2. Jesus is the Great Shepherd in His resurrection life *(Psalm 23).*
3. Jesus will be the Great Shepherd in His return *(Psalm 24).*

C. The Bridegroom of the Bride

1. Christ loved the church as His bride and gave Himself for it.
2. The bride (church) has an obligation to love the Bridegroom.

D. The Cornerstone and Foundation of the Building

1. Jesus is the Foundation upon which the church is built.
2. Jesus is the Cornerstone which gives the church its stability and strength.

E. The True Vine and the Branches

1. This may be the most intimate description of the relationship between Jesus and the church.

2. The vine is the total life of the branches.
3. Jesus' goal for our life is that we bear much fruit.

If Jesus loved the church enough to die for it,
will I love the church enough to serve in it?

____
(area of ministry which interests me)

Study 12 Outline

The Apocalyptic Names of Christ

"The Revelation of Jesus Christ, which God gave unto him, to shew unto his servants things which must shortly come to pass; and he sent and signified it by his angel unto his servant John" (Revelation 1:1).

John was a climactic writer. . . . Climactically, he wrote the last of the four Gospels. Climactically, he was the last person to write Scripture. Climactically, his Gospel is the greatest thesis on Christ. Climactically, his book was the last to be recognized as cannonical. Climactically, he wrote the last book of the Bible. Climatically, he wrote concerning the last things. (Elmer L. Towns)

Lesson Notes:

A. Jesus Christ
1. As our Prophet, Jesus is *the Faithful Witness.*
2. As our Priest, Jesus is *the First Begotten of the Dead.*
3. As our King, Jesus is *the Prince of the Kings of the Earth.*

B. His Eternal Completeness and Sufficiency
1. Jesus is the Alpha and Omega, everything from A to Z.
2. Jesus is the Beginning and Ending.
3. Jesus is the Lord who was, is and is to come.
4. Jesus is the Almighty.

C. The Son of Man
1. John saw Jesus as the Son of Man *in the midst of* the churches.
2. As the Son of Man, Jesus was exactly what the churches needed.
3. If people are going to see Jesus today, they will see Him in the midst of the churches.

D. The Lion and the Lamb

E. The Coming Conqueror
1. The Conqueror is described by the name *Faithful and True.*
2. There is at least one name of Jesus which no one knows.
3. Jesus conquers by His name *the Word of God.*
4. Ultimately, Jesus is the King of Kings and Lord of Lords.

F. The Root and Offspring of David

G. The Bright and Morning Star

Study 1 Discussion Sheet

The Name of Jesus

And she shall bring forth a son, and thou shalt call his name JESUS: for he shall save his people from their sins (Matthew 1:21).

How can I grow in the knowledge of the Lord?

Why should I grow in the knowledge of the Lord?

What is His name?

Title Name Office

What does "Jesus" mean?

How can I "live up to the name of Jesus"?

THIS WEEK IN THE WORD

[ ] Matthew 1

[ ] Matthew 2

[ ] Matthew 3

[ ] Matthew 4

[ ] Matthew 5

[ ] Matthew 6

[ ] Matthew 7

The Title "Lord"

For unto you is born this day in the city of David a Saviour, which is Christ the Lord (Luke 2:11).

Therefore let all the house of Israel know assuredly, that God hath made that same Jesus, whom ye crucified, both Lord and Christ (Acts 2:36).

That if thou shalt confess with thy mouth the Lord Jesus, and shalt believe in thine heart that God hath raised him from the dead, thou shalt be saved (Romans 10:9).

MAKING JESUS LORD	

HOW TO PREPARE A BOOK REVIEW

Book Title ____

Author ____

The thing I liked best about this book is______________________________

____

This book would be enjoyed most by______________________________

____

The major theme/message/impact of this book is______________________

____

____

On a scale of one to ten, I rate this book a __________.

THIS WEEK IN THE WORD

[ ] Matthew 8

[ ] Matthew 9

[ ] Matthew 10

[ ] Matthew 11

[ ] Matthew 12

[ ] Matthew 13

[ ] Matthew 14

Study 3 Discussion Sheet

The Office of Christ

Come, see a man, which told me all things that ever I did: is not this the Christ? (John 4:29).

How is Christ a prophet in my life?

How is Christ a priest in my life?

How is Christ a king in my life?

What is one thing I have in Christ which I can claim this week?

REPORTING ON A SPECIAL NAME GROUPING OF OUR LORD

1. Read chapter 3 in the book, *The Names of Jesus*, by Dr. Elmer L. Towns.
2. Identify one thing that impresses you most about the names in this grouping.
3. Choose a favorite name. Read how it is used in the Bible. Think of specific ways this name can be applied in the context of your life.

THIS WEEK IN THE WORD

[ ] Matthew 15
[ ] Matthew 16
[ ] Matthew 17
[ ] Matthew 18
[ ] Matthew 19
[ ] Matthew 20
[ ] Matthew 21

The Old Testament Prophetic Names of Jesus

Philip findeth Nathanael, and saith unto him, We have found him of whom Moses in the law, and the prophets, did write, Jesus of Nazareth, the son of Joseph (John 1:45).

And beginning at Moses and all the prophets, he expounded unto them, in all the scriptures the things concerning himself (Luke 24:27).

See chapter 4 of* The Names of Jesus *to complete the following:

OLD TESTAMENT NAMES	*NEW TESTAMENT MEANINGS*

My favorite Old Testament name for Jesus is ______________________________.

This name means ______________________________.

It helps me most because ______________________________

______________________________.

THIS WEEK IN THE WORD

[ ] Matthew 22

[ ] Matthew 23

[ ] Matthew 24

[ ] Matthew 25

[ ] Matthew 26

[ ] Matthew 27

[ ] Matthew 28

The Salvational Names of Jesus

For I know that my redeemer liveth, and that he shall stand at the latter day upon the earth (Job 19:25).

Let the words of my mouth, and the meditation of my heart be acceptable in thy sight, O LORD, my strength and my redeemer (Psalm 19:14).

See chapter 5 of* The Names of Jesus *to complete column 1.

SALVATIONAL NAMES	PEOPLE NEEDS

THIS WEEK IN THE WORD

[ ] Mark 1

[ ] Mark 2

[ ] Mark 3

[ ] Mark 4

[ ] Mark 5

[ ] Mark 6

[ ] Mark 7

Study 6 Discussion Sheet

The Birth Names of Christ

Therefore the Lord himself shall give you a sign: Behold, a virgin shall conceive, and bear a son, and shall call his name Immanuel (Isaiah 7:14).

For unto us a child is born, unto us a son is given: and the government shall be upon his shoulder: and his name shall be called Wonderful, Counsellor, The Mighty God, The Everlasting Father, The Prince of Peace (Isaiah 9:6).

Complete the following:

BIRTH NAME	*ITS MEANING TO ME*
Dayspring from on High	
Immanuel/Emmanuel	
Wonderful Secret	
Counsellor	
The Mighty God/El Gibbor	
The Everlasting Father	
The Prince of Peace	

THIS WEEK IN THE WORD

[ ] Mark 8

[ ] Mark 9

[ ] Mark 10

[ ] Mark 11

[ ] Mark 12

[ ] Mark 13

[ ] Mark 14

Study 7 Discussion Sheet

The Service Names of Christ

Even as the Son of man came not to be ministered unto, but to minister, and to give his life a ransom for many (Matthew 20:28; Mark 10:45).

Nothing "just happens" with God. As you complete the following, think about why Christ has these names and what they mean.

PEOPLE PROBLEMS	*SERVICE NAMES OF CHRIST*

HOW CAN I BE USED BY CHRIST TO MEET NEEDS?

My spiritual gift is: ______________________________.

My area of ministry interest is: ______________________________.

THIS WEEK IN THE WORD

[ ] Mark 15

[ ] Mark 16

[ ] Luke 1

[ ] Luke 2

[ ] Luke 3

[ ] Luke 4

[ ] Luke 5

The Sonship Names of Christ

I will declare the decree: the LORD hath said unto me, Thou art my Son; this day have I begotten thee (Psalm 2:7).

What similarities do you see?

LIKE FATHER LIKE SON

God is . . .	*Jesus is . . .*

THIS WEEK IN THE WORD

[ ] Luke 6

[ ] Luke 7

[ ] Luke 8

[ ] Luke 9

[ ] Luke 10

[ ] Luke 11

[ ] Luke 12

Study 9 Discussion Sheet

The Godhead Names of Christ

And Simon Peter answered and said, Thou art the Christ, the Son of the living God (Matthew 16:16).

THE ALPHA AND OMEGA

Make your own list of the names or attributes of Jesus by using each letter of the alphabet to correspond with the first letter of each word.

A –

B –

C –

D –

E –

F –

G –

H –

I –

J –

K –

L –

M –

N –

O –

P –

Q –

R –

S –

T –

U –

V –

W –

X –

Y –

Z –

Using the letters of your first name as an acrostic, list those names of Jesus from the list above which you will claim personally this week.

"One name cannot express all He is, and over 700 names cannot exhaust what He is." — Elmer L. Towns

THIS WEEK IN THE WORD

[ ] Luke 13

[ ] Luke 14

[ ] Luke 15

[ ] Luke 16

[ ] Luke 17

[ ] Luke 18

[ ] Luke 19

The Jehovistic Titles of Christ

Jesus said unto them, Verily, verily, I say unto you, Before Abraham was, I am (John 8:58).

If I were an animal, I would be a ______________________________ because ____.

I AM	*HOW JESUS IS THIS TO ME*

This week, I need Jesus to be my____.

THIS WEEK IN THE WORD

[ ] Luke 20

[ ] Luke 21

[ ] Luke 22

[ ] Luke 23

[ ] Luke 24

[ ] John 1

[ ] John 2

Study 11 Discussion Sheet

The Church Names of Christ

And I say also unto thee, That thou art Peter, and upon this rock I will build my church; and the gates of hell shall not prevail against it (Matthew 16:18).

PICTURES OF JESUS AND HIS CHURCH

See page 122 of The Names of Jesus.

If the Church is a . . .	*Then Jesus is a . . .*

Husbands, love your wives, even as Christ also loved the church, and gave himself for it (Ephesians 5:25).

If Jesus loved the church enough to die for it,
I ought to love the church enough to serve in it.

I would like to use my spiritual gift of ______________________ in this area of ministry:

______________________________. I need to call: ______________________

this week about getting involved.

THIS WEEK IN THE WORD

[ ] John 3

[ ] John 4

[ ] John 5

[ ] John 6

[ ] John 7

[ ] John 8

[ ] John 9

The Apocalyptic Names of Christ

The Revelation of Jesus Christ, which God gave unto him, to shew unto his servants things which must shortly come to pass; and he sent and signified it by his angel unto his servant John (Revelation 1:1).

FIND THE HIDDEN NAMES OF JESUS

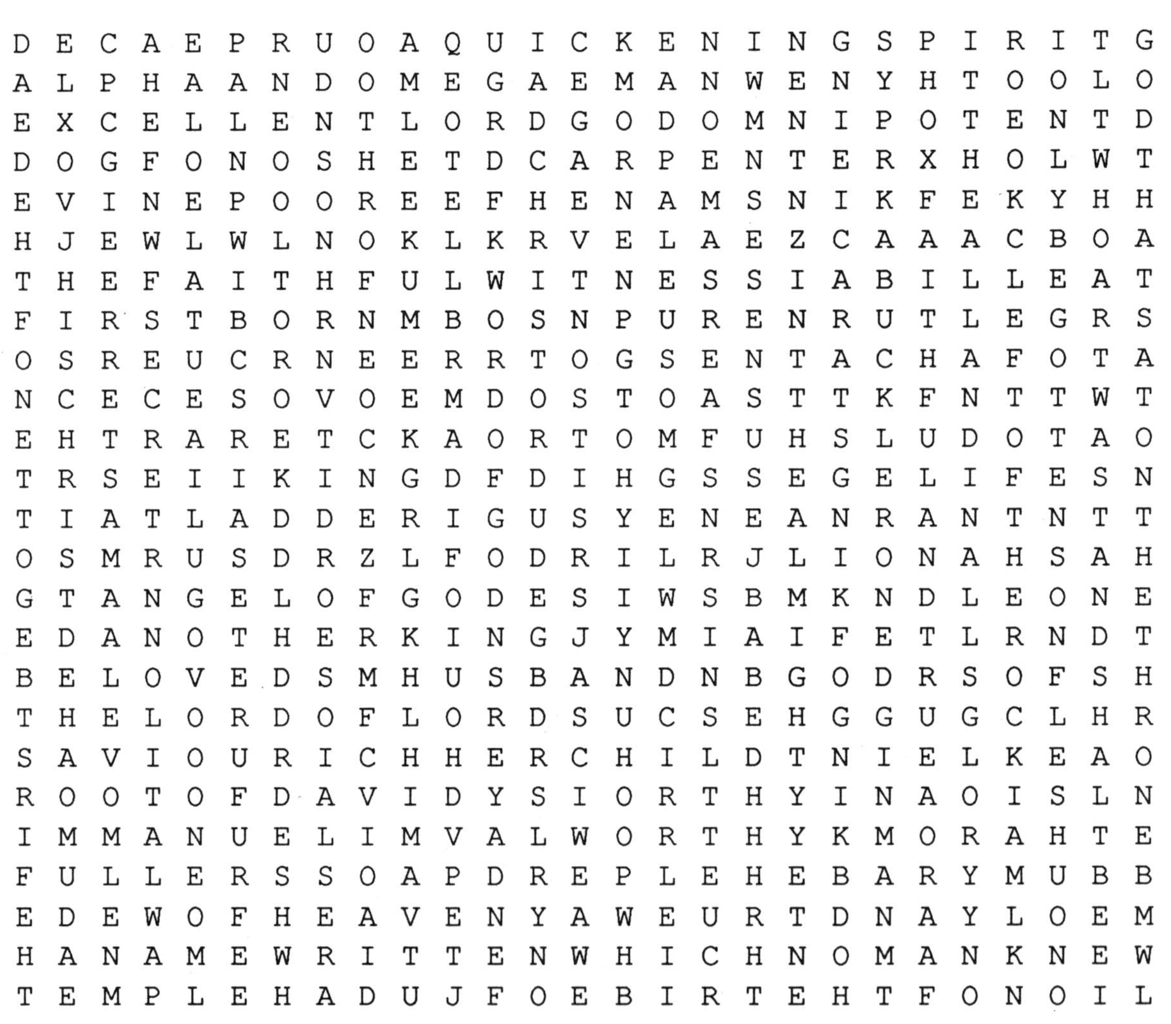

My favorite name of Jesus is ____.

This name emphasizes His ministry of ______________________________________.

I respond to this name by ____.

THIS WEEK IN THE WORD

[ ] John 10

[ ] John 11

[ ] John 12

[ ] John 13

[ ] John 14

[ ] John 15

[ ] John 16

Next week, take five more days to finish your reading of the Gospels!

FIND THESE HIDDEN NAMES IN THE PUZZLE ON PAGE 88

A Buckler
A Quickening Spirit
A Name Written Which No Man Knew
Alpha and Omega
Angel of God
Another King
Babe
Beloved
Brother
Carpenter
Christ
Cleft of the Rock
Dew of Heaven
Excellent
Faithful and True
First Born
Flesh
Glory
God
God That Sat on the Throne
Hen
Her Child
Husband
I AM
Immanuel
Jesus
Jew
King
King of Kings
Ladder
Life
Lion of the Tribe of Judah
Lord God Omnipotent
Man
Meek
One
Only Begotten Son
Peace
Poor
Pure
Root of David
Saviour
Sent
Sin
Son
Temple
The All and in All
The Almighty
The Faithful Witness
The First Begotten of the Dead
The Lord of Lords
The Son of God
Thy New Name
Veil
Vine
Who Art Wast and Shalt Be
Wisdom
Worthy

(Answer key on page 56.)

How to Keep a Daily Journal of Your Christian Life

by
Elmer Towns

Perhaps you know the feeling. You finally come to the realization of what it is God has been trying to tell you only to find out you could have learned that lesson days, weeks, or even months ago had you taken time to listen. "Is there something I could have done to learn this lesson faster?" you wonder. The answer, "Perhaps."

For several hundred years now, many Christians have used journaling as a means of disciplining themselves to examine their life and listen to what God is telling them. Some of these journals have become profound classics in evangelical devotional literature. Others have been examined by historians to help us better understand an era in our past. But all served their purpose in helping the journal writers listen more carefully to what God was trying to tell them.

Many Christians are reluctant to keep a journal because they do not perceive themselves as writers. They may not spell well, have poor grammar, or have difficulty writing in a consistent style. Actually, that is one of the advantages of journaling. Because you are the only intended reader of your journal, things like spelling, grammar and writing style are not as important as in other forms of writing, i.e. writing for publication. If you can read what you write, then you can write it in your journal.

The benefits of journaling are numerous. First, it helps fast-moving people slow down and notice the life around them they might otherwise miss. Second, it gives people an opportunity to record how they feel about the things that are happening in their life. Third, it provides a means of recording the important lessons God teaches us each day. Over time, a person's journal can record significant growth in his or her life which might otherwise go unnoticed and/or unmeasured. Also, a person may use the journal to record God's answers to prayers and other good gifts received from the Father.

How to Get Started Writing

The hardest step in any new discipline is the first step. It is far easier to decide to keep a journal next week than it is to journal today. But if you want to experience the benefits which can only be known through journaling, you need to take that first step today.

Remember, when you write your journal, you are writing for yourself. This gives you a great deal of liberty in how you do it. Some people purchase a special notebook or diary in which to write their journal. Others use separate sheets of paper and bind them together later. You may want to write your journal on a home computer. Some people have even used a cassette tape to record their journal, usually to be transcribed to paper later.

Begin by recording today's date. Then write about what you have been learning recently, what has been happening in your life, how you feel about that, and any other special concerns you may have. Some people find it easier to give their journal a name and write to the journal as they might converse intimately with their closest friend.

How to Keep on Writing

Many people begin a journal each year, but by February it is no longer in use. This problem can be overcome by viewing journaling as an opportunity rather than a duty. It is an opportunity to have a few quiet moments in each day when you can take time to look at what is happening in your life, listen to what God is trying to tell you, and think about what you should be doing in the days and weeks to come. It is easier to find time to do that than to find time for yet another meaningless activity we feel we "ought" to do.

Not everyone who keeps a journal makes daily entries. Your schedule may cause you to miss a day or two each week. On other occasions, you may find yourself making both a morning and evening entry in your journal. Don't quit if you miss a day. Simply pick up the next day and keep writing.

A Three-Month Plan for Journaling

You can make your study of the names of Jesus far more meaningful in your life by determining now to journal during the next three months. That may seem like a big challenge at the moment, but if you take it on one day at a time, you may be surprised with what the next three months have in store.

Begin your journaling time by reading a chapter from one of the four Gospels. You will read the four biblical accounts of the life of Christ as you study the many recorded names of Christ in Scripture. As you read the chapter for that day, ask yourself, "What does this chapter tell me about who Jesus is?" Choose a significant name or title of Jesus that summarizes your answer.

Start writing with the statement, "Today I believe God wants me to see Jesus as (insert your name for that day)." Then write about what has been happening recently in your life. Have there been times when you needed to see Jesus in the context of today's name? What about the day before you? Are there things in your schedule you would do differently in light of who Jesus is? Use these and other similar questions to help you apply the meaning of that day's name to your life.

Once a week, set aside time to read your journal for the past week. Do you see a pattern or trend in what God has been teaching you? Is there something you need to be especially alert to this week? Is there something specific you need to do in light of what you have been learning?